Moving to Adoption
Using the UEA model to help children move from foster care to adoption

Mary Beek, Elsbeth Neil and Gillian Schofield

Published by
CoramBAAF Adoption and Fostering Academy
41 Brunswick Square
London WC1N 1AZ
www.corambaaf.org.uk

Coram Academy Limited, registered as a company limited by guarantee
in England and Wales number 9697712, part of the Coram group, charity
number 312278

British Library Cataloguing in Publication Data
A catalogue record for this book is available from the British Library

ISBN 978 1 913384 10 4

Project management by Jo Francis, Publications, CoramBAAF
Designed and typeset by Helen Joubert Design
Printed in Great Britain by The Lavenham Press

For the latest news on CoramBAAF titles and special offers, sign up to
our free publications bulletin at https://corambaaf.org.uk/subscribe.

Contents

About the authors

Dr Mary Beek

Mary Beek is an Honorary Research Fellow at the Centre for Research on Children and Families in the School of Social Work at the University of East Anglia. She has had a parallel career in social work, mainly in the fields of fostering and adoption practice and management. Mary's research interests are in the lived experiences of foster care and adoption, and she has been involved in longitudinal studies of children growing up in foster care (with Professor Gillian Schofield), and of contact after adoption (with Professor Elsbeth Neil).

Based on their research, Mary and Gillian Schofield developed the Secure Base model of therapeutic caregiving, which is widely used in the UK and in diverse countries including China, Thailand, Vietnam and Ukraine, where Mary devised Secure Base training programmes to support the establishment of foster care as an alternative to institutional care.

Professor Elsbeth Neil

Elsbeth Neil is a Professor and Director of Research in the School of Social Work at the University of East Anglia. Her research interests are in how adoption is experienced by adoptees, birth relatives and adoptive parents, and particularly how birth and adoptive families keep in contact. She is also interested in understanding the support needs of all who are affected by adoption and the role of social workers in helping families.

Professor Gillian Schofield

Gillian Schofield is Emeritus Professor of Child and Family Social Work at the Centre for Research on Children and Families in the School of Social Work at the University of East Anglia, where she has taught social workers and conducted research since 1990. She was awarded an OBE in the Queen's Birthday Honours 2020 for services to children and family social work and fostering. Gillian has research interests in attachment and development, abuse and neglect, care and offending, LGBTQ young people in care, permanence in long-term foster care, and moving from foster care to adoption. She has published widely in these areas, including (with Mary Beek), the *Attachment Handbook for Foster Care and Adoption* (2nd edition, 2018) and practice guides on the Secure Base model (2014a, b).

Acknowledgements

Many people over many years have helped us to understand the significance of each child's move to adoption, and provided the impetus for the Moving to Adoption project and for this book. The project began with a consultation phase and we are grateful to the professionals, foster carers and adopters from all over the UK who were committed to supporting children's moves and who shared their ideas, experiences and practice innovations with us.

During the first phase of the project, Dr John Simmonds (Director of Policy, Research and Development, CoramBAAF) and Dr Danya Glaser (Visiting Professor at University College London and Honorary Consultant in Child and Adolescent Psychiatry at Great Ormond Street Hospital for Children) shared their wisdom and provided warm support and guidance, and we are grateful to them both.

The Moving to Adoption model was piloted in two local authorities – Norfolk County Council and the London Borough of Southwark. The pilot project involved adoption, fostering and looked after children's managers and social workers, foster carers and adopters from these areas and from other fostering and adoption agencies. Everyone involved showed deep commitment to the well-being of the children in their care and a willingness to explore change and to develop practice. Our sincere thanks for their participation and feedback.

Janet Barker (Adoption Team Manager) and Anne Murphy (PhD student, UEA) worked with the research team to disseminate the Moving to Adoption model to adoption agencies across the UK and to support implementation and gather feedback. In addition, their own practice-based feedback has been invaluable to the development of the model.

Input on the model's application in Scotland was helpfully provided by Rhona Pollock, Jane Steele and Robin Duncan from the Adoption and Fostering Alliance (AFA) Scotland.

Finally, we are extremely grateful to our funder, the Sir Halley Stewart Trust, which has supported us throughout the project. The views expressed within this book are those of the authors and not necessarily those of the Trust.

Introduction

For the majority of children adopted from care in the UK, adoption confers legal security, loving relationships and a sense of belonging in the adoptive family. These benefits can help the child to recover from early adversity and provide lifelong reassurance and support. In most cases, however, adoption also means that the child must be moved from a trusted foster family that has provided a secure base, where attachment relationships will have formed, and where the child is feeling settled and secure. In addition, adoption often means that the child loses key relationships with birth family members, along with their identity as a member of their birth family community. Each of these losses can have a lifelong impact.

Contemporary adoption, therefore, should be underpinned by policy and practice that both support the parenting capacities of the adopters, *and* respect the child's previous relationships and identities, actively seeking to mitigate the inherent losses faced by adopted children and adults. With this principle in mind, this book focuses primarily on the practice associated with a key phase of the adoption process – that of supporting the child to move successfully from their foster home to their new adoptive family. Positive practice during the move will take into account how children of different ages experience and make sense of the move cognitively, and manage it emotionally, so that adults can offer the most appropriate help and support.

Most children are aged under five years when placed for adoption. They will usually have lived in foster care for 18 months or longer before moving to their new parents. In traditional adoption practice, children typically moved between 5 and 14 days (according to the age of the child) after meeting their new parents for the first time. After the move, children often did not see their foster carers again for a period of several weeks or months after placement, and for some there was no further contact, although some adopters chose to remain in touch. This model remains in use in some agencies, but in recent years, practice has been evolving in different ways across the UK. Current practice therefore reflects a range of timescales for the move to take place and a variety of plans for contact with the foster carer, both before the formal matching and after the placement day.

Research has highlighted the importance of the quality of the move for the well-being of the child and the future stability of the adoption (Selwyn *et al*, 2015; Neil, Young and Hartley, 2018; Neil *et al*, 2020). A substantial minority of adopters in these studies reported difficult moves. Common difficulties included plans that were rushed or curtailed, stressful travel arrangements, and plans that were not child-focused and did not allow the child to come to terms with feelings of anxiety and loss. Both studies identified a statistically significant relationship between difficult moves and poorer adoption outcomes.

Additionally, there is professional uncertainty regarding whether or how contact with foster carers should be maintained after the move (Boswell and Cudmore, 2014; Meakings et al, 2018). Some agencies routinely plan a series of face-to-face and virtual contacts during the early days and weeks of the placement, diminishing in length and frequency. Others choose a more individualised approach, depending on the quality of the adult/child and adult/adult relationships. In some cases, a "clean break" with the foster family is felt to be necessary in order for the child to settle and build new attachments, although there is no research evidence to suggest that this is the case.

In summary, planning and supporting a successful move to adoption is a piece of social work practice that is recognised as vital for the future welfare of the adopted child. At the same time, there is professional uncertainty about how best to plan the move in a way that places the child's emotional needs at the centre, whilst also supporting the foster carers and the prospective adoptive parents.

In response to this situation, a practice development project took place between 2016 and 2018, at the Centre for Research on Children and Families, University of East Anglia (UEA). This project was conducted by the authors and funded by the Sir Halley Stewart Trust (Neil, Beek and Schofield, 2018). Two local authorities (Norfolk County Council and the London Borough of Southwark) worked in partnership with the UEA research team to pilot an adapted approach to moving children to adoption, developed from published literature and stakeholder engagement. The research team examined the professionals' experiences of this adapted approach and gathered feedback from the foster carers and adopters involved in the project. This led to the development of the UEA Moving to Adoption model.

From the outset, the Secure Base model (Schofield and Beek, 2005, 2009, 2014a, 2014b) was seen as foundational to an area of practice that relies on an in-depth understanding of the impact of children's earlier adverse experiences on their emotional development and their difficulty in forming trusting relationships in foster and adoptive families. The Secure Base model is already well established in fostering and adoption practice, with a range of online materials available to support both training and practice development. However, the model had not previously been applied to moving to adoption practice, so this project was a valuable way of using a familiar attachment-based model of caregiving to support the development of the new UEA Moving to Adoption practice model.

During 2019 and 2020, members of the research team delivered face-to-face and online training on the model to a wide range of individual and regional adoption agencies (RAAs) across the UK. Some weeks after the training, the team offered a follow-up consultation with a key professional from each agency, and gathered feedback on issues that had arisen around the implementation of the model. This feedback helped the team to develop advice and guidance.

The UEA Moving to Adoption model builds on existing good practice for moving children to adoption. It is not prescriptive in determining specific timeframes or plans for these moves. Instead, the model is governed by a set of principles within which a range of practice might occur. This focus on practice led by underlying principles rather than fixed procedures means that the model is responsive to specific conditions (for example, where the foster family and the adoptive family live far apart) and the full range of placements (for example, children of all ages, ethnicities and abilities). The key principles of the model are also relevant to the variations in legislative frameworks, policies and procedures across England, Wales,[1] Scotland[2] and Northern Ireland.

Additionally, the key principles and much of the practice recommended by the UEA Moving to Adoption model may be helpful when planning other moves that children must make, for example, from short-term foster care to a long-term foster care or special guardianship family, kinship care in Scotland or to other family and friends settings.

This Good Practice Guide introduces and explains the UEA Moving to Adoption model. The guide begins by reviewing the key messages from relevant research. Chapter 2 explores the ways in which the UEA Moving to Adoption model is underpinned by the theoretical framework of the Secure Base model (Schofield and Beek, 2014a, b). Chapter 3 examines the social work practice associated with preparing the child, the foster carers and the adopters for the child's move to adoption. Chapters 4, 5 and 6 explain the three stages of the UEA Moving to Adoption model and provide examples of how it can be applied in a range of situations. The final chapter of the guide covers suggestions for implementing and sustaining the UEA Moving to Adoption model in social work practice. The chapter concludes by considering the support needs of professionals engaged in the complex task of moving a child to adoption.

---

1   The UEA model is compatible with good practice guidance in Wales (see https://www.afacymru.org.uk/wp-content/uploads/2020/11/Transitions-PG_E.pdf).

2   In recognition of the distinct elements of the Scottish legal system, advice for practitioners in Scotland is included throughout this guide. Appendix 3 provides additional information on practice within the Scottish legal system.

NOTES ON TERMINOLOGY

Throughout this guide:

- The term 'adopters' will be used for approved prospective adopters, and may apply to either a single or a two-parent adoptive home.

- The terms 'foster carer' and 'foster carers' are used interchangeably, and may refer to a single carer or one carer from a two-parent household, or both carers from a two-parent household.

- The terms 'he', 'she' and 'they' are used interchangeably when referring to children.

Chapter 1
The theory and research background

Contemporary adoption in the UK usually involves the transfer of an infant or young child from a trusted foster family, with whom the child has lived for some months, to an adoptive family who (prior to the moving period) is previously unknown to the child or the foster carers. The child may or may not have had face-to-face contact with birth family members whilst in foster care, and this contact may or may not continue after the move to adoption. In all cases, when an adoption order is made, the child's legal tie to their birth family is terminated and full parental responsibility is conferred on the adopters. In certain cases, this can occur without the consent of the birth parents.

For all involved in the adoption, therefore – the foster carer, the adopters, the birth family and the child – there are fundamental shifts in relationships and identities. Previous ties will be weakened or broken, new roles and ways of life must be acquired. There will be opportunities and new beginnings and also uncertainty, loss and grief.

The complexity and far-reaching consequences of adoption mean that each step of the adoption process should be taken with the utmost care and evidence-based, whilst at the same time tailored to the individual circumstances of the case. Making the move from their foster family to their new adoptive family is a key step of the adoption process for each child and this chapter focuses on the theory and research that can inform practice at this stage. The experiences of children, foster carers, adopters and birth parents are explored in turn.

THE EXPERIENCES OF CHILDREN

Times of transition are stressful for all children, and children in care (even those who are very young) have often experienced multiple moves and changes of caregiver. The move to adoption may prompt difficult memories from the past or associations with previous traumatic moves. At the same time, the child will need to manage separation from the trusted foster carer and the loss of important foster family relationships, whilst also building trust in the new adoptive parents. Theory and research can help us to think carefully about how children might experience these moves and how best to respond sensitively to their needs and feelings.

Attachment, separation and loss

An understanding of the nature and significance of early attachment relationships is important in adoption practice. There is now well-established and widespread agreement that the quality of children's caregiving in their early months and years is key in providing a foundation for their emotional development and long-term mental health, although later changes in the child's caregiving environment, for better or worse, can nevertheless change a child's trajectory (Bowlby, 1951; Rutter, 1979; Howe, 2011; Schofield and Beek, 2018).

Bowlby (1969) suggests that selective attachments to primary caregivers develop from the age of about six months. From this time, children usually show a clear preference for one or more caregivers; when distressed, they will seek to be near this person, and even brief separation can provoke distress and protest. The permanent loss of a primary caregiver in childhood is traumatic for children of all ages, but has been identified as especially difficult to manage in the first three–four years of life (Rutter, 1971; Bowlby, 1980; Breier et al, 1988).

Children who enter the care system have usually experienced adverse caregiving in their original families and are likely to have insecure attachments to their birth parents, but they will nevertheless experience a sense of loss of birth parents and other family members, including siblings. There is evidence that in these circumstances, a relationship with a sensitive and committed secure base foster carer can be therapeutic in building security and resilience and improving outcomes (Schofield and Beek, 2009; Dozier et al, 2011). However, separation from this secure base relationship will involve further losses for the child and, depending on how it is managed, may have medium and longer-term implications for the child's well-being, particularly for those aged over 12 months (Gauthier et al, 2004).

Theory and research suggest, therefore, that when a child is to be moved from a foster carer to a new adoptive family, the move should be managed with the utmost care and with an informed understanding and sensitivity to the child's developmental needs. This means building on the progress towards health and security already made in the foster family, while also taking account of their earlier experiences of trauma, attachment insecurity, separation, loss and grief.

Children's development: thinking and feeling

Infants and young children develop increasingly sophisticated ways of engaging with the world from birth onwards, as they move from sensory experiences to active play, using language and learning about social relationships. Sensitive support from caregivers will help them to make sense of their experiences and the associated feelings. An understanding of the child's developmental stage in terms of thinking and feeling can help to shape plans for the move to adoption that are attuned and responsive to the child's inner world.

Children aged under three years (the most common age range for placement from care into adoption) can feel the absence of their foster carer when they move to adoption, but they will have limited capacity to understand the reasons for the separation. Children who are moved at this age, therefore, are likely to experience strong feelings, but they will find it hard to articulate these feelings, or to make sense of them.

Further development occurs at the age of three to four years, when children can begin to take the perspective of their caregiver into account, and can rely on mental representations of them as well as accepting care from others to cope with brief separations. These developments may in theory help a child to cope with a move to adoption, but if the child has experienced exposure to adverse parenting, trauma or multiple separations, this is likely to have had a negative effect on their emotional and cognitive development. They are therefore more vulnerable and more likely to experience fear, an acute sense of abandonment and negative memories of past separations (Bowlby, 1980; Lanyado, 2003; Hindle and Schulman, 2008; Burnell *et al*, 2009). Therefore, all pre-school children in care will struggle to understand why they are moving to a different family and find it hard to manage emotionally. Many older children who are placed for adoption will also struggle to understand the reasons for their move (Thomas *et al*, 1999). But with the support of their foster family, they can be helped to think about the positive implications of their future life in the adoptive family.

For caregivers and professionals, there is a further complication, as children do not always show their feelings directly (Dozier *et al*, 2005). For example, some children who are angry or worried become controlling or rejecting towards adults who are trying to care for them. Some children avoid their painful feelings and appear not to care that they are moving to a new family, or may seem excited and keen to move quickly (Lanyado, 2003). Even babies and young toddlers who are already vulnerable may defend themselves by cutting themselves off from their emotions, appearing outwardly compliant and apparently unaffected by separation (Ainsworth *et al,* 1978; Howe, 1998, 2011).

When children's outward behaviour is not congruent with their feelings, adults may make the wrong interpretation. For example, it is very easy to mistake the lack of shows of emotion and over-compliance for "resilience" (Boswell and Cudmore, 2014). Research with foster carers and babies has shown that if babies demonstrate self-reliant behaviour in distressing situations, carers may withhold nurture, feeling that the baby does not want or need it (Stovall and Dozier, 2004).

Children who show little outward signs of emotion during their move to adoption can, therefore, be perceived as "fine", and difficult underlying feelings may not be taken into account (Boswell and Cudmore, 2014). Caregivers may be also be dealing with their own intense emotions at this stage (Lynes and Sitoe, 2019) and so find it harder to tune in to those of the child. Caregivers or professionals who are in touch with the child's difficult feelings may find it hard to raise the subject, for fear of spoiling the "positive direction of travel" (Boswell and Cudmore, 2014).

It is essential that children are helped to express the full range of their feelings, both positive and negative, and that they receive support with these feelings if they are to recover from their losses and rebuild trust. This is important before, during and after a move to adoption (Lanyado, 2003; Hindle and Shulman, 2008; Browning, 2015; Schofield and Beek, 2018). If the grieving process is not supported, feelings of unresolved grief can emerge some time after the move, later in childhood or even in adolescence (Fahlberg, 1994).

Although it is important not to minimise the impact of the loss and separation when children move from foster care to adoption, children whose feelings are acknowledged and who are well supported by their foster carers can respond well to the dedicated care and lifelong commitment on offer from their adopters, and settle well. So all those involved need to keep a careful balance between being aware of the child's potential anxiety and distress, while at the same time building on the child's potential for trust and forward progress.

Supporting a child's move to the adoptive family

The child's loving and trusting relationships with the foster carers form the foundation of a positive move to adoption. These relationships are therapeutic in that they can help children to recover from early harm, promote healthy development and support future attachment relationships (Schofield and Beek, 2018). The Secure Base model (Schofield and Beek, 2014), discussed in more detail in Chapter 2 of this practice guide, provides a framework for understanding the positive impact of these relationships and the ways in which they can support the child before, during and after the move to adoption.

There has been little research into the role of foster carers, especially after the child has moved. Research into children separated from their primary caregivers for hospitalisation, however, suggests that the ongoing presence of an existing attachment figure, remaining available and continuing to have a supportive role, can reassure and help children, rather than cause confusion as had previously been thought (Bowlby, 1980; Robertson and Robertson, 1989).

There is professional uncertainty regarding visits from the foster carer to the child after the move to adoption. Some professionals have promoted early and frequent contact, while others have delayed or ended the contact, feeling that it would be confusing to the child and that a "clean break" was needed (Boswell and Cudmore, 2014, Meakings et al, 2018).

Overall, a gradual transition process, which acknowledges the losses involved for the child and includes the ongoing but decreasing involvement of the foster carer, has been identified as key in helping children to make a positive move to adoption (Aldgate and Simmonds, 1988; Breier et al, 1988). Browning (2015) also proposes that the impact of the move can be "softened" for the child by a gradual transition process with slowly decreasing contact with foster carers, overseen by a well-functioning professional team. This fits with what we know of children's cognitive and emotional development, in that time needs to be allowed and support offered for children to manage anxiety and build trust.

THE EXPERIENCES OF FOSTER CARERS

At the heart of the transition process from foster care to adoption is the nature of the foster carer's relationship with the child and the role of the foster carer in supporting the child before, during and after the move.

Foster carers in all short-term placements begin by caring for a child about whom there is likely to be a great deal of uncertainty. This uncertainty will surround the child's developmental difficulties and how amenable to change they might be in the context of good quality care *and also* in terms of possible placement outcomes, ranging from return home to placement for adoption. In this context, the carer's role is to build a relationship with the child, providing a secure base that will help the child recover from harm and from separation from the birth family. This will maximise the child's healthy development, in order to benefit from whatever placement direction may be taken. Once an adoption plan is confirmed by the court, this focuses attention on matching and the move to a new family. The carer's therapeutic role and relationship with the child prior to that decision will be the foundation for this important next step.

Ambiguities are intrinsic to the role of foster carer, particularly the potential tension between the roles of "professional carer" and "committed parent" (Schofield et al, 2013; Blythe et al, 2014). Research suggests that both of these roles are important and should be integrated, as children need carers who are both knowledgeable and skilled but also sensitive and loving. This integration is particularly necessary in pre-adoption placements where the foster carer role is to offer security, love and commitment (often from birth) to a child whom they will then need to support in the move to another family (Kirton, 2001; Blythe *et al*, 2014).

Feelings of grief and loss are commonly reported by foster families when fostered children move on, but can be exacerbated when transitions are unexpected or when carers feel uninvolved or powerless in decision making (Edelstein *et al*, 2001; Riggs and Willsmore, 2012; Höjer *et al*, 2013; Blythe *et al*, 2014). Lynes and Sitoe (2019) identify the grief that foster carers experience as "disenfranchised", meaning that it often cannot be openly shared, and therefore acknowledged and supported by friends and professionals. Foster carers in this study reported that social workers, peers or family often did not understand that they had loved the child "as their own", and some felt that they needed to hide their grief as they could be deemed to be behaving unprofessionally or not permitted to foster again. In some cases, the depth of feelings was so hard to bear that they decided to "hold back" emotionally from future foster children, or to cease fostering altogether.

Other research (Pyman, 2007) found a range of different responses from foster carers to the task of supporting a child's move to adoption. Some carers in this study, as also found by Lynes and Sitoe (2019), found it difficult to manage their emotions because they saw the child as their own, while others reported holding back emotionally, arguing that this protected both the infant and themselves from feelings of loss. But the Pyman research found that some foster carers cared wholeheartedly and lovingly for the child, but then managed their feelings of grief and loss when the child moved to adoption by defining this as part of their role and also as their gift to the child – to love them and then to help them move on to a new adoptive family. These carers demonstrated the capacity to integrate loving and letting go, using cognitive strategies to manage the emotional commitment and the loss of a child positively. This was based on their knowledge of the child's needs and their clarity about the rewards and job satisfaction of their role when it led to a successful adoption placement for a vulnerable child who needed a permanent family. This constructive framing of their experience could be supported by partners and other family members and reflected on with the support of a supervising social worker.

THE EXPERIENCES OF ADOPTERS

Adopters come to the point of the child's move to join their family after what can be a long and often difficult journey, both prior to approaching the adoption agency and during the process of assessment, preparation, approval and waiting for the match. Emotions need to be processed about this route to parenthood; these may include feelings of loss mixed with positive and excited anticipation, and also anxiety about the child to be matched with them and how well their new family will work. All of this will need ongoing reflection with support from social workers in order to manage the fresh emotional rewards and challenges of becoming adopters.

The process of being matched to a child, meeting and getting to know them, and welcoming the child into their home can be a very positive experience, but for some adopters it has been identified as "significant but problematic" (Lewis, 2018). Adopters in this study described rigid social worker planning for the moving period, which did not always take into account the perspectives of the adopters, the foster carers or the child. There was tension between the emotional event of meeting their child for the first time, and the bureaucratic and "business-like" procedures around this.

Sims (2020) also refers to the "matrix of tensions" around the transition period, during which the adopters must negotiate the highly individualised process of becoming a parent in the context of a strictly regulated and collaborative process. The adopter is required to be both creative (for example, to make a "welcome book" for their child), but also compliant (for example, one adopter was told that the book must contain images of a specific toy that the child enjoyed). The feeling of being under scrutiny but at the same time unsure of what was expected of them caused further tension for some adopters (Lewis, 2018).

Blackmore et al (2020) focus on the "materials" that foster carers and adopters are required to produce (photo books, audio materials, videos, and so on) aimed at helping the child move across the "bridge" to adoption. The use of the materials by the foster carers was variable, with some claiming that there was "no point", or that "the child was too young to understand". This could be indicative of the foster carers' unmanaged grief and often had an adverse effect on the eventual move. Good sharing tended to lead to a good relationship later on, with the carers actively supporting the adopters' connection with the child. This positive approach was consistent with that described by a focus group of foster carers associated with the UEA pilot study (Neil, Young and Hartley, 2018), many of whom had actively developed memory books to record the child's life in the foster home and to take with them to the adoptive home.

The early weeks of an adoption placement can also involve a complex mix of positive and difficult feelings and responses for adopters. As well as happiness and excitement, feelings of anxiety, loss of identity, loneliness, disappointment, low mood and physical symptoms are common. Post-adoption depression is now a recognised condition and the risk of developing it is as high for adoptive mothers as for birth mothers in the general population developing post-partum depression (Senecky *et al*, 2009).

Post-placement depression may be linked to adopters' unrealised and perhaps unrealistic expectations. For example, they may expect to be fully in control of the adoption process, to rapidly achieve a loving relationship with the child, to be warmly supported by all their friends and family, or to have a child who is responsive to and "healed" in a fairly straightforward way by their care. If these and other hopes are dashed by the initial reality of the situation in which they find themselves, this can lead to profound disappointment and despair. Difficult feelings may be denied or underplayed, as they can be hard for adopters to share with a social worker who has steered them through the process and championed them as "good parents". Some adopters who experience these feelings may fear that the child will be removed (Foli, 2009).

Meakings and colleagues (2018) examined the support needs of adopters during and immediately after the move and found a universal need for services, even amongst adopters of very young children, who had been described as "straightforward". Many adopters of children beyond babyhood were finding it hard to feel close to their children. Some felt that the child's close relationship with the foster carer was affecting the way the child felt about the adopters, while others described divided loyalties with birth family members. The child's early adversity and inadequate preparation for adoption were also seen as problematic. Areas of need for support included:

- support and guidance with emotional and behavioural issues, and concerns about children's physical well-being and developmental progress;

- support with strengthening adoptive family relationships;

- help to manage and improve relationships with siblings in the same placement and also with adoptive siblings.

In terms of the role of foster carers, research by Neil, Young and Hartley (2018) reported that adopters found it helpful when foster carers:

- were friendly, welcoming and encouraging;

- passed on detailed information about the child;

- had relevant information about adopters to prepare the child;

- were willing to stay near the adopters' home during the introductory period;

- gave practical advice, and parenting tips as needed.

The issue of contact between the foster carers and the adopters and child during and immediately after the move has been described by some adopters as problematic and by others as supportive and helpful (Meakings et al, 2018; Neil, Beek and Schofield, 2018). In some cases, adopters have viewed the visits as distressing for the child, and emotionally charged for them and the foster carers. However, other adopters have felt that foster carer visits were a pleasant and natural extension of the introductory period and helpful to the child in demonstrating that the foster carers had not "disappeared" or forgotten about them. Even if the child was upset, some adopters felt that the contact was beneficial as it provided a window into the child's sense of loss and opportunities for them to be comforted and reassured.

Support from significant family members is very important for adopters, both through their journey to adoption and once the child is placed. Some agencies have advised their adopters to minimise or avoid visits from family and friends during the early days and weeks after the child has moved to them, with the aim of allowing them to focus solely on the child and promote an attachment relationship (Lewis, 2018; Meakings et al, 2018). Some adopters have valued this time and space to focus on the child without additional pressure and distraction. Others, however, have found this advice to be unhelpful, denying them badly needed practical and emotional support from their network and creating a "pressure cooker" like atmosphere in the household (Lewis, 2018). A balance needs to be struck between allowing plenty of relaxed time for the child and adopters to establish their relationships as a family, and opportunities for selected key members of the wider circle of family and friends to meet the child and offer support, with an emphasis on avoiding any situation that might risk overwhelming the child. There is a case here for individualised plans, developed well ahead of the move, which take into account the particular needs of the child as well as those of the adopters.

THE EXPERIENCES OF BIRTH RELATIVES

Although the adoption order will extinguish the legal tie between the child and the birth parents, and other relatives, they will continue to be part of the child's identity, and in many cases there will be significant relationships to be supported through a range of contact arrangements (Neil and Beek, 2020). An understanding of the experiences of birth relatives before, during and after the child's move to adoption can help to inform practice that allows birth relatives to feel respected and understood, and that can maximise their potential to make a positive contribution to their child's life in the adoptive family.

Historically, the majority of research in this area focuses on birth mothers who have relinquished infants to adoption. There is much evidence that these parents experience a profound and life-changing loss that may impact across the lifespan, and intensify over time (Winkler and van Keppel, 1984). Logan (1996) found that many birth mothers reported intermittent depression linked to feelings of guilt, anger, sadness and grief, and one-third of women in this study had been referred for specialist psychiatric treatment.

Research in the UK that looks specifically at birth parents' experiences of being compulsorily separated from their children has identified four key themes (Neil *et al*, 2010; Schofield *et al*, 2011; Schofield and Beek, 2014; Mermarnia *et al*, 2015).

- **Isolation.** Birth parents commonly feel isolated, unimportant and marginalised at the time the decision for adoption is taken and moving plans are being made. They report a lack of support to help them to improve the situation, and a sense that their side of the story was not listened to, that unfair evidence was used against them in court and that their emotions were seen as unimportant in the overall picture.

- **Disconnection from emotion.** Birth parents may at times appear to be disconnected from their difficult feelings. They may use a matter-of-fact tone when describing highly distressing events and minimise the reasons why their child was removed. Guilt and shame may lead to a disconnect between what is shown on the outside and what is felt internally. Alcohol and drugs may be used to numb or block difficult feelings. Minimising feelings in this way may enable birth parents to create a narrative about the loss of the child that is bearable both for them to live with internally and to present to others.

- **Re-negotiation of identity.** The loss of the child can involve the profound loss of a sense of self and of identity as a parent. For some, this can promote a need to "move on" that denies the impact of the loss, including having another child. For others, there is an unresolved struggle between being a parent and yet not being able to enact that role. Parents may also seek to deny or minimise their own role in the child's abuse or neglect (Neil *et al*, 2010; Mermarnia *et al*, 2015), possibly in an attempt to try to manage their "spoiled identity" (Goffman, 1963). In some cases, birth parents are able, over time and with support, to repair their parenting identity and/or to build a new identity through contact with the child or in a different, positive role.

- **Ambiguous loss/disenfranchised grief.** Many birth parents describe a confused grieving process, sometimes referred to as "ambiguous loss", since the child has gone from their life, and yet still exists, and in some cases there may be ongoing contact: the child is physically absent from the birth parent, and yet has a strong psychological presence. Grief may also be "disenfranchised", since others may not know about the loss or understand the depth and pain of it. Ongoing contact with the child may help to resolve some of these feelings over time. But it can also present further challenges, with birth parents reporting that contact meetings can engender feelings of inadequacy, uncertainty and anxiety that the child will not remember them or want to see them.

The majority of birth parents describe the adoption process as an unfair, hostile and alienating experience and one in which they had very little power to influence events (Neil *et al*, 2010; Mermarnia *et al*, 2015). The legal process leading to adoption is often adversarial and unpleasant and has a traumatic emotional impact for the birth parent (Neil *et al*, 2010). Parents can feel helpless in a powerful system where there is "no one in my corner", as one parent described: 'These people have got so much power, and they can ruin your life like that [clicked fingers]. In a snap' (Mermarnia *et al*, 2015, p. 306). By the time children are legally adopted, there may be little semblance of a working relationship between birth parents and social workers, this having consequences for the child as the involvement of birth parents in planning to meet the child's identity needs may not be possible (Neil *et al*, 2010).

After adoption, birth parents can struggle to move forward with their lives. They may be worn down by feelings of shame, worthlessness or guilt; as one birth mother said, the adoption had made her feel 'like you are no good for nothing' (Neil *et al*, 2010, p. 162). Birth parents can be left with a sense of hopelessness and worthlessness that stops them attempting to improve their situation or accept help from others, and future relationships with adults and children can be negatively affected. These experiences highlight the need for sensitive professional practice as well as advocacy (including legal advocacy) and independent support before and after the adoption.

Four key areas of helpful practice have been identified by birth relatives (Neil *et al*, 2010):

- **Honesty and openness.** Even when there was difficult information to be shared, birth relatives valued social workers who provided this information clearly and honestly, shared written copies of what had been said and gave details and evidence to support the information. Social workers were also appreciated for being clear about what needed to change, not giving false hope and keeping promises.

- **Availability and reliability.** Birth relatives valued social workers who returned their calls and responded readily to their questions and requests. Having a consistent, named social worker was also very much appreciated.

- **Being kept informed, involved and consulted.** Many birth relatives found the meetings and events leading up to the adoption to be bewildering and confusing. They valued timely information, and a sense of being included in decision-making in some way. Specifically, they mentioned having some agency in the selection of prospective adopters and being able to contribute to life story books and later life letters.

- **A sensitive, supportive attitude.** Birth relatives appreciated social workers who recognised and acknowledged the personal pain that they were feeling, who made time to listen and who showed "humanity and decency" in their approach. Personal gestures from the social worker, such as acknowledging the death of a parent with a card, were mentioned and valued by birth relatives.

CONCLUSION

Research on the experiences of children, foster carers, adopters and birth relatives highlights both the range of those experiences and the importance of learning lessons for practice from both the more negative and the more positive experiences of children's moves to adoption. Each move involves a unique constellation of personalities, circumstances, hopes and fears. Professionals must be sensitive to the individual nuances of each case, whilst also drawing from the breadth of knowledge generated by research and theory.

Chapter 2
Using the Secure Base model to support a successful move to adoption

In developing the UEA Moving to Adoption model, it was important both to focus on how each child's development would link with their thinking and behaviour around the move, and also to think about the tasks, opportunities and challenges for professionals, foster carers and adopters as they work together to support the child's move. To help with this, it made sense to use a developmental framework that was already familiar to many practitioners: the Secure Base model, which draws primarily on attachment theory and therefore has a particular value in supporting a successful move to adoption.

For many years, attachment theory has provided an important framework for understanding children's healthy development and what they need from parents and other caregivers in foster care and adoption in order to feel secure and fulfil their potential. Also very important for child placement social work has been the understanding from attachment theory of the potentially long-lasting impact of early parenting that has been harmful or traumatic for the child, the impact of separation and loss, and the role of therapeutic caregiving in bringing about change and recovery. Attachment theory links well with other developmental theories, such as resilience theory, and so has an important contribution to make to developing practice in moving to adoption and relationship building in both the foster and adoptive families.

The Secure Base model is drawn from theories of attachment and resilience combined with research in child placement. It outlines five dimensions of therapeutic caregiving that help the child to heal, recover from difficult histories and build new, trusting relationships. The principles of the Secure Base model are well established when applied to caregiving within the care system, but this is the first time that the model has been applied to supporting children's moves to adoption, and it is key to the understanding and implementation of the UEA Moving to Adoption model.

This chapter explains how and why the Secure Base model can support practice at each stage in moving a child to adoption. Using the structure of the model's five secure base dimensions, the text focuses on the detail of the child's development and on their thinking, emotions and behaviour as they leave their trusted foster family and build trust in a new adoptive family. The range of thinking and feeling of foster carers and adopters through this process is also considered, and helpful caregiving responses are described, along with the impact that these may have on the child's thinking and feeling. In this way, the Secure Base model provides practitioners with the key concepts and also a helpful form of words to explain to foster carers and adopters *why* certain kinds of caregiving approaches are recommended. For example, sensitively supporting the child to share both their positive and more difficult feelings and to accept comfort during the move will help the child to feel that their feelings make sense and can be managed, and this is likely to have longer-term consequences for the child's well-being in the adoptive family.

This chapter begins by setting out key concepts in attachment theory, and then the Secure Base model is briefly outlined, with each caregiving dimension explored in relation to aspects and stages of the move from foster care to adoption that make up the UEA Moving to Adoption model.

CORE CONCEPTS IN ATTACHMENT THEORY AND THEIR RELEVANCE FOR CHILDREN MOVING TO ADOPTION

Children moving from foster care to adoption are likely to bring with them feelings of anxiety connected with particular experiences of separation and loss. These may include moves of household and losses in the birth family, the move into care and, for some children, moves within care. As discussed in the previous chapter, concern about underestimating the impact of loss involved in moving to adoption was a major factor driving the need to explore new ways of managing the move.

In addition, children's early care may have been negatively affected by a range of parental difficulties and stresses such as trauma in their own childhood, mental ill health, drug or alcohol misuse, often compounded by socio-economic deprivation. Caregivers may have:

- rejected the child's emotional needs;
- responded unpredictably;
- been frightened or frightening.

In these situations, children may develop defensive strategies for coping and attempting to get their needs met that reflect their insecure attachment; for example, shutting down on feelings, being emotionally demanding, or becoming controlling or being passive in their relationships with caregivers.

Insensitive and unresponsive parenting can have a profound effect on children's expectations of self and others, and children may come to believe that:

- I am unlovable.

- Other people cannot be trusted to care for me.

These negative expectations of the self and others are referred to in attachment theory as "internal working models". They can change over time, but because they are deeply rooted in experiences of parenting, they can be resistant to change. Negative beliefs may also intensify when the child's anxiety is raised, for example, by removal from their birth family and placement in an unfamiliar foster family, but also during the move to the adoptive family. The child's emotional and behavioural development may be further adversely affected by these experiences of loss, and they will need a therapeutic environment in both the foster home and the adoptive home to support their recovery and make positive progress in feeling secure.

THE SECURE BASE MODEL

The Secure Base model of therapeutic caregiving was created by Gillian Schofield and Mary Beek at UEA (Schofield and Beek, 2014a, 2014b, 2018). It is based in attachment and resilience theory, but also draws on their child placement research. Therapeutic in this context means the day-to-day sensitive caregiving that helps the child heal, recover from difficult histories and thrive. Materials for the model are available on a free to access website.[3] The model helps practitioners, foster carers and adopters to understand each child's developmental needs and the corresponding caregiving approaches that promote security and resilience.

The Secure Base model underpins all aspects of the UEA Moving to Adoption model and is relevant at each stage of the child's journey. Initially, the Secure Base model can be used to help foster carers to understand and respond to the child's needs on entering care and throughout the placement, as they contribute to planning for and

---

3   https://www.uea.ac.uk/groups-and-centres/centre-for-research-on-children-and-families/
    secure-base-model

preparing the child for the move to adoption. The model can also support adopters in understanding the impact of the child's history and responding to the child's needs during the move, and once the child is building relationships with them as part of their family. In addition, it offers social workers a framework for understanding and engaging with the child, and for supporting both foster carers and adopters through the complex tasks and feelings that are involved in a successful move from foster care to adoption.

The Secure Base model outlines five dimensions of caregiving, each associated with a particular developmental benefit for the child:

- Availability – helping the child to trust.

- Sensitivity – helping the child to manage feelings.

- Acceptance – building the child's self-esteem.

- Co-operation – helping the child to feel effective.

- Family membership – helping the child to belong.

The first four dimensions are drawn from attachment theory as set out by Bowlby (1969) and Ainsworth *et al* (1971, 1978), and are associated with secure attachment. Schofield and Beek (2014) added an additional dimension, family membership, that completes the model. A sense of belonging is relevant for all children, but can be particularly challenging for those who are separated from their birth families and those who are moving to new foster or adoptive families.

It is important to bear in mind that the dimensions are not entirely distinct from each other. In the real world of caregiving, they overlap and combine. For example, a caregiver who is playing with a child in a focused, child-led way may be doing so with sensitivity and acceptance, as well as demonstrating availability and promoting co-operation. Similarly, the child's capacity to trust will contribute to expressing and managing feelings more successfully. However, it is necessary to assess and work with each dimension separately as well as together, as carers and adopters may have greater strengths in some areas than others, and children's development and needs on each dimension will also benefit from targeted understanding and support.

These caregiving dimensions and the connections between them are represented in Figure 1.

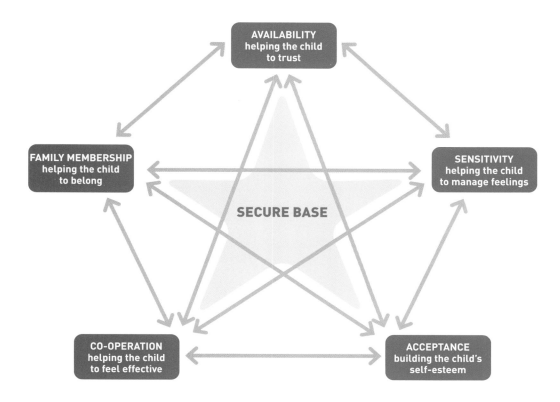

Figure 1: The Secure Base model

Each Secure Base caregiving dimension and each developmental benefit has relevance for a child moving to adoption, with the child's age, stage and history taken into account.

THE CAREGIVING CYCLE

It is important for foster carers and adopters to think about caregiver–child interactions as having the potential to shape the thinking and feeling and ultimately the behaviour of the child. These interactions underpin each of the five dimensions of the Secure Base model and are represented in the caregiving cycle (Figure 2).

The caregiving cycle begins with the child's needs and behaviour and then focuses on what is going on in the mind of the caregiver. How a caregiver *thinks and feels* about a child's needs and behaviour will determine their *caregiving behaviours*. The foster carer or adopter may draw on their own ideas about what children need or what makes a good parent from their own experiences or from what they have learned from training or preparation. The caregiving behaviours that result convey certain messages to the child. The child's *thinking and feeling* about themselves and other people will be affected by these messages and there will be a consequent impact on their *development*. This process is represented in a circular model, *the caregiving cycle*, that shows the inter-connectedness of caregiver/child relationships, minds and behaviour, as well as their ongoing movement and potential for change.

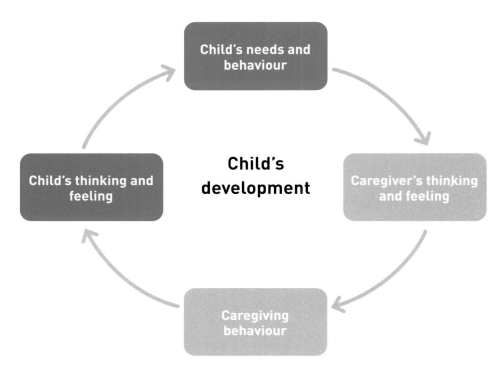

Figure 2: The caregiving cycle

The caregiving cycle encompasses the many interactions of family life. For infants and children of all ages, these range from the moment-to-moment exchanges, for example, at a mealtime, to managing major emotional distress or behavioural crises. Each interaction conveys a number of messages to the child and has an incremental effect on their developing beliefs about themself, beliefs about other people, and the beliefs about relationship between self and others in the world around them. Making these beliefs, these internal working models, more positive will influence the child's development and functioning in relationships, in the foster family, during the move to adoption and in the adoptive family. It will also go on to support the child's relationships with children and adults outside the family and capacity for play and learning at school.

AVAILABILITY – HELPING THE CHILD TO TRUST

Figure 3: Availability – helping the child to trust

This dimension focuses on the caregiver's ability to convey to the child a strong sense of being physically and emotionally available to meet their needs, both when they are together and when they are apart. When the caregiver can offer this, consistently and in a range of circumstances, the child begins to trust that their needs will be met warmly, consistently and reliably. Anxiety is reduced and, over time, the child gains the confidence to explore the world with pleasure, safe in the knowledge that care and protection are there if needed. While in foster care, the availability of the carer will help the child to make progress in their capacity to trust, whatever their history. The challenge is then to maintain that emerging capacity for trust during the move to adoption and while the child is settling in the adoptive family.

The child's needs and behaviour

Infants and young children in foster care with a plan for adoption are likely to have lacked consistently available care and protection from birth family caregivers. They may also have experienced more extreme forms of neglect or abuse that will have made it particularly difficult for them to trust adults and may therefore be wary of them. Children from such difficult backgrounds present a range of challenges to foster carers and adopters. A high degree of availability is likely to be needed in order for children to make the developmental progress that will enable them to thrive in foster care, move successfully and build trust in their new adoptive family.

Infants and young children in care will have often experienced parents or other birth family caregivers who will have reacted to their expression of needs and distress with frustration, anxiety and rejection. Often caregivers may have been intermittently and unpredictably available, "blowing hot and cold", because of their own unmet needs or the external pressures in their lives. Uncertainties about the availability of a safe adult will cause children to have anxieties around caregiving. In particular, children who do not receive emotionally available parenting will find it difficult to experience themselves from birth as lovable or to engage with any pleasure in the world around them. They will find it hard to trust that an adult will be available or that their needs will be met at all, let alone consistently, safely and kindly. Most detrimentally, previous caregivers may have reacted to a needy child with unpredictable anger or frightening aggression, causing the child to feel deep fear, panic, confusion and helplessness. The child is then likely to associate closeness with feelings of fear and dread, and feel panicked by the approach of any potential new caregiver, however trustworthy they may be.

These deeply rooted experiences may lead young children to distance themselves from their caregivers, or constantly demand attention or be determinedly in control. These defensive strategies associated with insecure attachment, which were learned and necessary for survival in the birth family, can become problematic, stressful or hurtful to caregivers who want to nurture, soothe and help children recover from their difficulties. This will be a challenge to both foster carers and adopters. Even if the child has made some progress in developing trust while in foster care, defensive strategies may still be triggered by the anxiety of moving into a new adoptive family or by later challenges such as starting school or making friends.

Caregiver thinking and feeling

The challenge for caregivers in providing availability for a child with difficulties in trusting adults is a complex one. The eventual goal is to change the child's expectations of adults – to convince them that they *can* trust and rely on adults to care for them safely and meet their needs.

Firstly, however, caregivers may have to disentangle some confusing messages. From small babies to pre-school and older children, their behaviour and, later, words may be indicating, 'I don't need you, I can look after myself', or 'I need you all the time, but you can never be available enough for me', or 'I can only manage my anxiety about being rejected by trying to be in charge, controlling you and everything that happens in the family'.

Foster carers and adopters at all stages in building their relationship with a child may have to remind themselves of the true needs that lie behind these messages. This is no easy task, particularly when the depth of need may be expressed in the form of resistant or hostile behaviour. Caregivers may need additional support, therefore, to help them to *think* about and reflect on this particular child's previous experiences in relationships and ask themselves, **What does *this* child expect from adults?**

Most important at this stage in the availability cycle, however, is the capacity of the caregiver to generate *flexible theories* about what is going on for the child. For example, upset behaviour at bedtime may be linked to wanting the caregiver to find their favourite cuddly toy, or to a memory of a previous traumatic experience, or a combination of the two. A willingness to try different approaches to explaining the child's thinking and behaviour is necessary, often starting with the simplest explanations, and working patiently for small changes.

In the light of this reflection on what is going on in the child's mind, the caregiver needs also to think in a more focused way about the question, **How can I show *this* child that I will not let them down?** Trust-building availability and interventions can then be targeted to the child's needs more precisely and adapted over time. The process of helping the child to manage trust vs distrust will have begun in foster care, but may last through childhood in the adoptive family, as new challenges present themselves, so the need for flexible thinking about the child's behaviour and mind will continue.

Caregiving behaviour

With a better understanding of the sources of a child's difficulty with trust, caregivers can begin to be more **alert to their child's needs and signals**, and then take opportunities to do and say things that will begin to change the child's internal working model, their negative expectations of themselves and adults. Available caregivers will need to give both **verbal and non-verbal messages of availability**. But – and this is perhaps the greatest skill of secure base caregiving – they will need to find ways of doing this that feel comfortable and acceptable to the individual child, such as knowing when to move closer for a cuddle and when to wait for a child to make the first move. This is particularly crucial when caring for infants and young children as it requires observing and tuning in to the child, only offering physical comfort and closeness in the ways and at the pace the child is comfortable with. If the child experiences closeness as overwhelming or intrusive, they are more likely to shut down and resist it, physically or emotionally.

Foster carers will need to develop these approaches to availability differently for each child, and can help adopters with their experience and ideas about what has previously worked best for the particular child. But young children in foster care and moving to adoption will be changing developmentally, as they age chronologically, as they recover from previous difficulties and adapt to moving to a new family. So adopters will need to undertake their own process of observing, listening and learning the approaches to availability that will help to build the child's trust in them over time.

The child's thinking and feeling

As children begin to *trust* that close adults are not going to disappear or let them down, their thinking will begin to change in subtle ways. They will begin to gain a sense of **I matter, I am safe, I can explore and return to my secure base for help**, and, crucially, **other people can be trusted**.

As anxiety is diminished, the drive to explore, learn and play is freed up. There will be increasing confidence and competence to venture away from the secure base and discover the wider world – but there will also be an increasing capacity to rely on caregivers for comfort, nurture, guidance and to enjoy appropriate closeness. Signs of progress in these areas may be painfully slow to appear, but they are among the most exciting and rewarding for caregivers in foster care and adoption to observe.

When the move to adoption is being planned, the stage that the infant or child has reached in relation to trust in the availability of key caregivers while in foster care will need to be carefully assessed. This will help with preparing the adopters and planning the move to maximise the continuity of support and availability.

SENSITIVITY – HELPING THE CHILD TO MANAGE FEELINGS

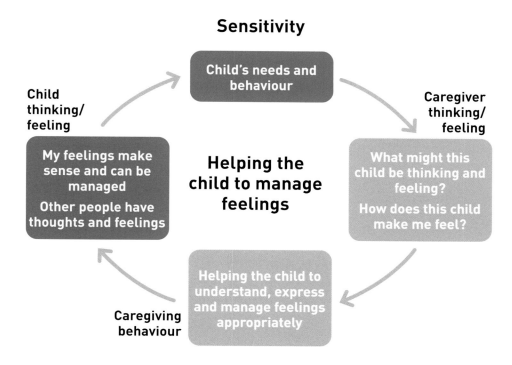

Figure 4: Sensitivity – helping the child to manage feelings

Sensitivity, in this context, refers to the caregiver's capacity to "stand in the shoes" of the child, to think flexibly about what the child may be thinking and feeling and to reflect this back to the child. The sensitive caregiver also thinks about their own feelings and shares them appropriately with the child. The child thus learns to think about and value their own ideas and feelings and the thoughts and feelings of others, and is helped to reflect on, organise and manage their own feelings and behaviour.

For foster carers, tuning in to the child's thinking and helping them to express and manage their feelings will be key to promoting their healthy development and pleasure in their world, but also in planning the move and supporting the child in expressing and managing their feelings during the move to the adopters.

For adopters, tuning in to the child's thinking and feeling as they hear about, meet and get to know the child will play an important part in helping to ensure the child's emotional comfort with the pace and timing of this developing new relationship, both during and after the move to their family.

The child's needs and behaviour

Many infants and children in foster care come from difficult backgrounds where they have lacked opportunities to have their thoughts and feelings acknowledged and understood. They may have been in situations where there was no adult able or available to help them deal with strong feelings, so anxiety, anger or despair may have overwhelmed them at times, including when physical needs were not met. Infants and young children who have been emotionally neglected, frightened, hungry or some combination of these will become profoundly anxious. Children may also have had caregivers who denied their feelings, suggesting, for example, that they should not need a cuddle so often. This can lead to the child failing to trust their feelings. Sometimes, children will have been cared for by adults who could not manage and regulate their own feelings, and children may have been blamed or feel themselves to blame for chaos or violence in the household. For a range of reasons, previous caregivers may have been too anxiously absorbed with their own distress or too preoccupied with their own needs to attune themselves to the feelings and minds of their children.

Lacking the resource of a safe and containing adult mind or a supportive scaffolding for managing their feelings, children develop their own ways of coping with them. This might involve letting feelings go excessively, using feelings to control others, holding feelings in, or denying that they exist at all. Each strategy is problematic in a family relationship setting in foster care or adoption where feelings are normally communicated fairly openly, in a managed and regulated way within trusting relationships.

Foster carers and adopters, as well as social workers, will therefore need to be aware of the sources of the child's difficulties in expressing and managing their feelings appropriately, and the strategies the child may have previously adopted to cope. It can also be expected that for many children the strong and often mixed feelings – some of anxiety, some of hope – associated with the move to adoption may lead to a child reverting to previous coping strategies and needing extra support to be able to communicate those feelings, put them into words and accept reassurance.

Caregiver thinking and feeling

For foster and adoptive caregivers caring for a child who has just joined their family, a primary task is to reflect on and make sense of the child's complex feelings and behaviour. They must attempt to tune in to this child, stand in the child's shoes and try to imagine, **What might this child be thinking and feeling?** They need to be particularly thoughtful about the child's previous experiences and flexible in their thinking about how these might have shaped the child's thinking processes and expression of feelings. Although it is painful to do so, the capacity to project oneself into the mind of a child who has been maltreated is important. It is from this starting point that caregivers can begin to think about the child's beliefs and expectations of themself and others, and to reflect on how this might connect with their current behaviour.

The caregiver thinking will not only be about what is in the child's mind about the past – it will also be about making sense of the way in which the child will be reacting to daily small events. The trauma of aspects of the child's history and the impact of the child's anxieties and dysregulated feelings on carers in the present can, if not fully understood, negatively affect the mind of the caregiver and the positive atmosphere of the family. In this context, it is essential for caregivers to have a containing relationship with a thoughtful, reflective social worker, who can bear thinking about the child's difficult history and current behaviour, accurately, without distortion and without being overwhelmed. They should also be able to allow the caregiver to reflect honestly on the question, **How does this child make me feel?**, and make connections both to the child's past experiences and their own past experiences that may trigger certain emotions.

Foster carers, adopters and social workers, reflecting separately and together on how the particular child's move to adoption can best be planned and supported, will need therefore to reflect on the mind of the child and how this move may be experienced; in particular, the child's potential anxieties about separation and their hopes and worries about whether the new family can accept their feelings, in order to love and care for them.

Caregiving behaviour

With this framework for reflection in place, and with the availability of supportive social workers, caregivers can begin to adopt a range of approaches geared towards helping a child to **understand and express and manage their feelings appropriately**. An important first stage is that of *naming feelings*, helping the child to reflect on them, recognise them and think about their origin. Even for preverbal infants, it can help to put into words the caregiver's sense of what lies behind behaviour – the sadness or anger or hunger – as the words may be recognised over time and the feelings will be mirrored in the gentle, calming tone of voice.

Often the child's expression of feelings is either suppressed or excessive, and caregivers must help some children to show feelings more freely, and others to communicate them in more constructive ways, using words or gestures, approaching the caregiver for a hug or pointing out the toy that they cannot reach.

In order to help children to understand and respond to the feelings of others, caregivers need to feel comfortable in expressing and discussing the full range of their own feelings. They are then in a position to model the fact that both positive and negative feelings can be safely managed. In particular, they can show children that *mixed feelings* are "normal" and that combinations of love and anger, longing and distrust, anxiety and eager anticipation are part of the human condition – affecting not only them but also their birth parents, foster carers, adopters, friends and social workers. Discussing the mixed feelings of characters in story books or on television can be helpful opportunities for learning.

Foster carers providing short-term care to an infant or child can usefully work with social workers to identify parenting approaches that can help them manage the child's feelings and cope productively with the most difficult areas of behaviour or times of day. These therapeutic caregiving goals can be discussed with the social workers, monitored for even small signs of progress and revised as necessary. For both foster carers and adopters, it is essential that these discussions are practical and lead to suggestions for day-to-day care, often around sleeping, feeding, playing or offering comfort, that can be tried out, with social workers available on the phone or email for quick follow-up discussions of successes or the need to learn from experience and adjust.

This learning process can not only inform the moving to adoption support plan; it will also give adopters some important ideas for what may work best when they need to continue what will be a gradual process of helping the child move towards a healthy capacity to express and regulate their emotions.

The child's thinking and feeling

The emotional education provided by sensitive caregivers enables the infant or child to discover that **my feelings make sense** and **I can manage my feelings**, gaining confidence that a range of feelings are appropriate and will not become overwhelming to themselves or others. Finally, the child can be helped to understand that **other people have thoughts and feelings** that must also be understood and taken into account in order to build mutually rewarding relationships.

As the child's thinking shifts and develops in these important ways, feelings become better regulated, and there is a likelihood of more constructive relationships, greater empathy, and more pro-social rather than antisocial behaviour. This process will have started in the foster home, but progress towards healthy development will have depended not only on the child's age, history, length of placement and level of difficulty in this area, but also on the foster carer's ability to tune in sensitively to this particular child and to support the adopters to do the same.

ACCEPTANCE – BUILDING THE CHILD'S SELF-ESTEEM

Figure 5: Acceptance – building the child's self-esteem

This dimension describes the ways in which the caregiver is able to convey that the child is unconditionally accepted and valued for who they are, for their difficulties as well as their strengths. This forms the foundation of positive self-esteem, so that the child can experience themselves as worthy of receiving love, help and support, and also as robust and able to deal with setbacks and adversity. This area of caregiving builds on the dimensions of availability and sensitivity. Children need to have started to learn to trust and to manage their feelings and behaviour in order to believe caregivers' praise and to take up opportunities that are on offer. On the other hand, early positive experiences that build self-esteem can also support the development of trust and emotional self-regulation.

It is very important that each infant or young child's sense of self-worth and what supports it is taken into account when planning and supporting the move to adoption. Any change involving a loss of relationships or living environment can have an impact on a child's sense of self and self-esteem. In the longer term, the move to adoption will offer opportunities for the child to build self-esteem in a settled family, but the moving process will represent a challenge that needs to be thought through and sensitively managed to help children who may otherwise slip back into self-doubt to continue to feel valued and accepted.

The child's needs and behaviour

Many children who come into foster care have a profound sense of worthlessness and low self-esteem, often complex and deep-rooted in origin. Their early parenting may have lacked warmth and acceptance. For some children, family life may have been frightening at times, and children may have been labelled negatively or scapegoated. The tendency of young children to see themselves as having a magical responsibility for negative events can lead them to experience themselves as "bad" and deserving of rejection.

Low self-esteem for children may also be connected with multiple separations and losses of familiar people and, for some children, compounded by the stigma and sense of difference incurred by being fostered or adopted. Children, therefore, may have deep-seated doubts about their fundamental "goodness", whether or not they "deserve" loving care and whether or not they will receive it if they are needy or behave "badly".

Children who do not have an internal working model of close adults as warm and accepting and themselves as loved and loveable will find it hard to face the world with confidence. They have not learned that they can be both "good" and "bad", "clever" or "not so clever", and yet still be accepted and valued. They often believe that if they cannot be the best, then they must be the worst. The danger, then, is that a child becomes trapped in a negative cycle in which they expect failure or rejection and so behaves in ways that are likely to produce this outcome.

These complex feelings become very relevant when children are facing major changes in their lives, including moving from a foster family to an adoptive family. Doubts about whether the foster carer really loved them or whether the adopters may also decide not to keep them may trigger historic feelings of doubt about their value and lovability. Hence, there is a need for reassurance in many forms from foster carers, adopters and social workers.

Caregiver thinking and feeling

Foster carers and adopters must hold in mind the sense that **this child needs me to value and accept them** – whatever the stresses of caring for the child may be. Alongside this, and especially if caring for the child is challenging, a caregiver must remember 'I need to value and accept myself' – so that their own self-esteem and emotional resources do not become depleted. This will be a key area for support workers. Caregivers who are feeling overwhelmed by their child's needs and finding it hard to parent positively may need to be reminded of their strengths and skills and helped to understand what factor or event in the child's history may be making it difficult for them to settle, and what might therefore be helpful parenting approaches.

By modelling acceptance of both strengths and difficulties in the caregiver, support workers can convey the message, 'You do not have to be perfect'. This will be alongside providing caregivers with advice, discussion and training that will help them to understand and accept the child's emotions and behaviour, identify targeted caregiving approaches and become better able to parent positively.

In the context of moving to adoption, there needs to be a shared understanding that the child's anticipation of the move, and the move itself, may trigger a return to some troubled behaviours reflecting low self-esteem that it was thought had been overcome. The child's progress can be recaptured, but the confident management of the move and good communication between the foster carers and adopters can reassure the child and make building and maintaining their self-esteem more likely.

Caregiving behaviour

With support, foster carers and adopters can build a range of skills and strategies for **helping the child to feel good about themselves and to manage setbacks**. Difficult behaviour can be approached in ways that do not undermine the caregiver's own self-esteem or that of the child. The positive message to the child is, 'Nobody is good at everything, but everybody is good at something'. So there is a focus in this dimension on activities and interactions that both enable children to feel positive about themselves, and also help caregivers to gain or regain a sense of being competent parents.

This positive, accepting approach does not mean that behaviour difficulties are not challenged, or that goals are not set to reduce behaviours that limit the child's progress and damage their relationships. On the contrary, it is critical for children, especially older children, to be and feel accepted not only in the family, but also in their peer group and the wider community. Caregivers, therefore, have to manage a careful balance between accepting children as they are, helping them to value and express themselves, *and* helping them to change aspects of behaviour that can threaten their acceptance by and relationships with others.

The child's thinking and feeling

The goal is for children to begin to think **I am accepted and valued for who I am. I do not have to be perfect in order to be loved and valued**, by my foster family or my adoptive family – or by friends and adults outside the family.

For some children, learning to accept themselves will always prove difficult, even with the most sensitive and accepting care, but self-esteem is so critical to healthy development that even small degrees of progress need to be worked for.

When a child moves from foster care to adoption, the aim will be for the adopters to build on the input by the foster carers and the child's increasing ability to accept and value themselves. Protecting the child's more positive internal working model will involve setting positive goals for the move and for the child's future in the adoptive family, while reducing any negative impact of the moving process. This is best achieved by generating for the child a continuous feeling of acceptance and being valued by all significant people in their lives – the foster family, the adoptive family, birth relatives, the professional network – and, for some children, in the wider community of nursery or school.

CO-OPERATION – HELPING THE CHILD TO FEEL EFFECTIVE

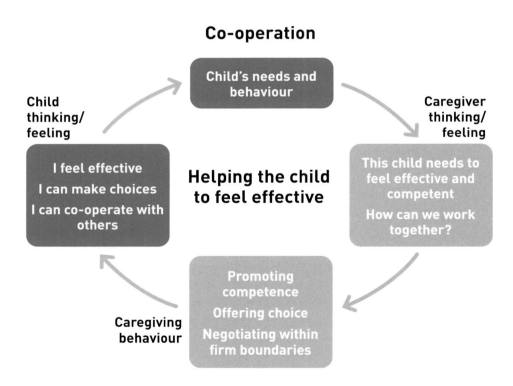

Figure 6: Co-operation – helping the child to feel effective

Within this dimension, the caregiver thinks about the child as an autonomous individual whose wishes, feelings and goals are valid and meaningful and who needs to feel effective. The carer, therefore, looks for ways of offering choices and promoting autonomy, but also working together in partnership and achieving co-operation with the child wherever possible. This helps the child to feel more effective and competent, to feel confident in turning to others for help, when necessary, and to be able to compromise and co-operate.

The benefit of focusing on this dimension for the child moving to adoption includes ensuring that the child feels that they are involved and have some influence over what happens. This includes, especially for non-verbal infants, confidence that their behaviour and communications are understood and responded to; for example, being given a favourite toy to hold if they seem anxious when meeting the adopters.

The child's needs and behaviour

Children coming into foster care have often not experienced this co-operative approach to parenting as part of their early care. Birth family caregivers may have been stressed by the demands of everyday life as well as parenting, and become over-controlling and intrusive, unable to allow the child the opportunity to make choices, feel competent and be effective. Birth parents may also have felt threatened by a child's need for autonomy and lacked the skills or capacity to negotiate, resulting in parenting behaviour that could be harsh and abrupt or passive and ineffective. Additionally, in many disadvantaged households there are fewer practical resources and less parental time for play, fun and enjoyable co-operative activities.

For a range of reasons, therefore, children may not have developed a sense of themselves as competent individuals, nor of adults as co-operative partners, either in exploration and play or in managing difficulties. As a result, a child may become passive and over-compliant in their relationships with adults, or may seek excessive control over them and also other children.

Toddlers and young children of the ages most likely to be in foster care with an adoption plan are particularly likely to assert themselves in ways that caregivers sometimes struggle to manage and to get the balance right between supporting the child's growing competence and setting limits. It can be difficult for carers, adopters and social workers to distinguish between "normal" toddler and pre-school behaviour and maladaptive behaviour that reflects a more troubled past and that may be exacerbated by the experience of uncertainty about the move. This can also challenge the move itself, when co-operative approaches are important, so trust in the foster carer is a crucial foundation.

Caregiver thinking and feeling

Most caregivers would understand that all children need to feel effective and competent, and would know that children should enjoy and benefit from opportunities to act on their environment, make choices and take gradual steps towards independence, even in early childhood. But children who feel ineffective and unsafe and who try to control caregivers can behave in ways that trigger difficult feelings in their caregivers, making it harder for them to work towards these co-operative goals and more likely that battles for control will dominate the relationship.

In many cases, therefore, foster carers and adopters will need help, especially in the early days of the placement, to take a step back to consider 'How is this child affecting my sense of effectiveness and competence?'. For caregivers, understanding their own experiences and the extent to which they need to be in control or are finding it hard to feel in control can be an important first step in co-operative caregiving. Shared reflection with social workers about the child's earlier experiences of caregiving and the ways in which issues of competence and control might have been handled with the child in the past, in the birth family and in previous placements, can also be helpful for the current caregiver. This leads to a stronger position from which to address the questions, **How can I help this child to feel more effective and competent?** and **How can we work together?** The caregiver is then able to take a step back, pause for thought and think in terms of forming a co-operative partnership with the child in order to achieve their shared and separate goals.

Because most children with a plan for adoption are pre-verbal infants and young children, achieving a sense of co-operation and helping them to feel less powerless and more competent requires some flexible and creative thinking.

Caregiving behaviour

In co-operative caregiving, there are two important areas of parenting activity. The first is to help children to learn that it can be safe and rewarding to act for themselves. To achieve this, caregivers will need to actively structure an environment that **promotes competence and choice**, providing opportunities for the child to feel genuinely effective. At all times, sensitive caregivers must be mindful of the delicate balance between facilitating the child's appropriate use of support and promoting appropriate independence. But for young children, it is very important to promote their sense of competence, for example, around feeding themselves or finishing a jigsaw puzzle, while offering support.

The second task for caregivers is to help children to experience co-operative relationships in which each partner contributes to the other's goals. The message to the child is that the tasks they are undertaking can be achieved by working on their own and/or with help from the caregiver. There will also be situations where the child can help out an adult; even toddlers like helping to set the table or finding their caregiver's slippers. These shared activities involve **making co-operation enjoyable**; actively demonstrating that sharing and working together can be rewarding and fun. At the same time, **negotiating within firm boundaries** ensures that safe and reasonable limits are set and comfortable compromises can be reached when necessary.

For infants and young children, experiencing themselves as having an influence on their environment in relation to the move to adoption will be limited to some degree by the constraints of their mental and verbal abilities. But nevertheless, they can be listened to and experience a sensitive response from attuned caregivers, which includes sharing information. When even very young children are being prepared for the move to adoption, there are many practical ways in which the child can be engaged in the process of introduction. These might include: showing the child a photo of the person who is visiting or whom they are seeing that day; offering a reminder of their name and role (e.g. social worker, adopter, birth grandparent); involving the child in putting biscuits on a plate for the visitor; choosing what toy to take to birth family contact; or sharing a photo of the adopters and the house that the child is being taken to visit, while holding a toy that was a present from them. These strategies treat the child with respect, enable them to feel more in control and that the world makes sense and is not random. They also allow opportunities for the child to express emotion, and can reduce anxiety.

The child's thinking and feeling

The foster carer and adopter must bear in mind that the child will need to have a developing trust in a secure base before they can feel safe enough to try new things, to make choices and to accept help when needed, or offer help to others. Only when the foundations of trust are in place will the child be able to take the risk of thinking and behaving differently, being assertive but also co-operative. A growing sense of effectiveness will help the child to know that **I can make things happen within safe limits**. And positive experiences of working together with trusted adults will develop the sense that it is rewarding to **compromise and co-operate**.

During and after the move to adoption, the child will benefit from the co-operative approach that is developed between foster carers, adopters, professionals and, where appropriate, birth relatives. This will increase the likelihood that the child's needs and perspective will be taken fully into account, will model co-operation, and also increase the child's sense that this move is a supported and positive change in their life.

FAMILY MEMBERSHIP – HELPING THE CHILD TO BELONG

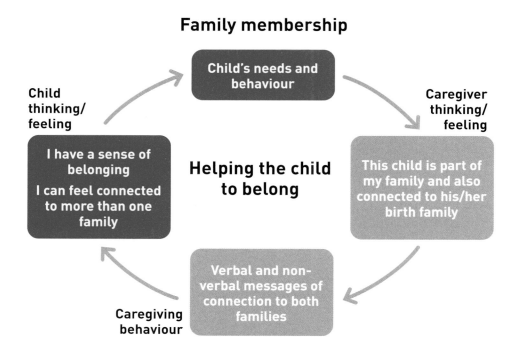

Figure 7: Family membership – helping the child to belong

Family membership is a vital strand of healthy emotional and psychosocial development. A child who has no close family relationships will carry feelings of psychological and social dislocation in our family-focused society. In contrast, the certainty of unconditional family membership can provide anchorage and the reassurance of practical and emotional support throughout life, acting as a secure base for exploration, identity and personal development.

When children are first separated from their birth families, the family membership dimension includes the capacity of the foster carer to include the child, socially and personally, as a full family member, while at the same time helping the child to maintain or establish an appropriate sense of connectedness and belonging to their birth family. In this way, the child can start to develop a comfortable sense of belonging to more than one family and a more coherent identity. This will support their sense of identity into the future, whether the next step is to return home or to a family member, remain in long-term foster care or move to an adoptive family.

Whether a child is in a short-term foster family or adoptive family, there will be an important task of managing their membership of the birth family in a positive way. During a child's move from foster care to adoption, the carers, adopters, birth parents and professionals need to help the child to manage the identification with and membership of at least three families.

For infants, the challenge is to creatively enable the child to hold on to these multiple connections, often in practical and sensory ways, using familiar toys or photos, for example. For older, more verbal children, there will be the need to share life story work that includes both their life within the birth family and their life in the foster family. For some children, there may be a final face-to-face contact with birth relatives in the period when they are also preparing to leave the foster home. The impact of the child's sibling relationships in the birth and foster family and their loss will also need to be recognised and managed. A sense of all the child's past and future family identities will need to be held in mind by all the adults to help the child develop a continuous and coherent self during and after the move to the adoptive family.

The child's needs and behaviour

Each child separated from their birth family will bring a unique set of experiences of family life, and each of these experiences will have shaped their expectations of their environment in the foster family, their anticipation of the adoptive family and their sense of what it means to be a family member.

It is important to remember that for most fostered children, there will have been some good times in the birth family as well as difficult ones, positive experiences and memories as well as sad or perhaps frightening ones. For all children, the challenges of adapting to a new family life in the foster family and subsequently the adoptive family are enormous. Depending on their age and understanding, all children will be grappling with different types and degrees of loss (of people, places, pets and friends), uncertainty (I've moved before so how long will I stay? Do they really want me?) and anxiety (Will I be safe? Will I fit in? Will I be loved?). The simple tasks of getting up in the morning and having breakfast in an unfamiliar family home can be mountains to climb for a child. It is hard to overestimate the potential stresses and strains that are involved in making the move initially into a foster family and subsequently an adoptive family, while managing complex feelings of loss and strong but often mixed feelings about the birth family.

The wider questions of identity and belonging, including class, ethnicity and religion, will also be affecting the impact on the child of moves between houses and families whose cultures and practices, as well as physical environments, may be unfamiliar.

Caregiver thinking and feeling

At the point of the move to adoption, the foster carers' and adopters' thinking and feeling needs to accommodate a high degree of flexibility about a child's sense of belonging in different families and how that is likely to change. The nature of the child's family memberships at this point in time will vary according to the age of the child, how the plan for the child has evolved, and the quality of relationships in the birth and foster families and those just developing in the adoptive family.

A child in foster care who moves to adoption will often have had a fairly close involvement with birth family members in the early weeks or months of their foster care placement prior to the decision being made about the longer-term plan. But during that time, they will also benefit from being treated as a valued part of the foster family. So the foster carers will need to think actively about the child's experience of their birth family identity and contact and how that is likely to be affected if face-to-face contact reduces or ceases on adoption. Adopters will also need to have information about and consider the child's previous significant relationships within the foster family and birth family.

What is important in all cases, therefore, is the capacity of the foster and adoptive family networks both to welcome children as new members, and also to be thoughtful, reflective and open towards the individual child and their birth family. The thinking is therefore complex, since it involves foster carers accepting that **this child needs to feel part of our family as well as connected to/feel part of their birth family**. For adopters, this thinking will also be about simultaneously holding the powerful and sometimes conflicting ideas that **this child needs to become part of our family but is likely to have important connections to their birth family and previous foster families**.

Caregiving behaviour

For foster carers and adopters, the primary task is to provide an environment that is emotionally warm, physically comfortable, accepting, supportive of its members, and that sets clear but reasonable expectations for shared living as a family. The variations within this framework are enormous and span the full range of culture, class, language, social norms and religious practice. It is here that we see a clear link to attachment theory, since sensitive caregivers provide this sort of welcoming environment, and have the capacity to be *reflective* in relation to the child's needs and feelings about the idea of belonging to a family.

Sensitive caregiving in this family membership dimension for foster families caring for a child who will be moving to adoption, therefore, involves seeking opportunities to provide **verbal and non-verbal messages of inclusion in both foster and birth families while preparing**

a child to move and belong to an adoptive family. Foster carers will be managing the present network of family relationships while looking to the future on behalf of the child. Adopters will also be giving **verbal and non-verbal messages of inclusion in their family**, managing the child's current and anticipated future relationships, but also looking back on the child's behalf to take account of significant families and family members to whom the child remains connected.

Caregivers for the child in this period, from coming into foster care to settling in an adoptive family, will need to employ a range of practical ways of supporting the child's understanding of and engagement with the changing reality of their family relationships and networks. These connections and changes can be discussed in many ways with infants and children (as described in subsequent chapters), using familiar clothes, toys and in particular photos. These must be sensitively adapted to the child's (often changing) needs and circumstances, with the aim of helping the child to feel a coherent sense of identity in what may be a complex network of relationships.

The child's thinking and feeling

The combination of inclusion in the current foster or adoptive family and the recognition of the possibility of being a member of more than one family, with different families playing different roles in their life, can enhance the child's felt security – 'I am safe and secure in this family, but I can also think and talk about how it feels to be a member of another family.' Over time, this will allow children to process their complex feelings, recognise and express different and mixed feelings and manage their dual or sometimes multiple memberships at a level that feels compatible with their particular circumstance, wishes and feelings. They can move towards a position where their thinking and behaviour reflect a coherent sense of self and acceptance that **I have a sense of belonging and can feel connected to more than one family**.

Caregivers who think flexibly and inclusively about a child's significant family ties and relationships are particularly valuable for supporting the thinking and feeling of a child in care who is moving into an adoptive family, especially when the child has a history of moves in the birth family and/or in care. Some foster carers may hold negative views of the birth family and will need help to manage the messages they give to the adopters. On the other hand, some foster carers become familiar with the birth family through supervising contact, and, when this has gone well, they may be able to help adopters to think more positively and flexibly about accepting the child's connection to the birth family.

42

CONCLUSION

As this account suggests, integrating the Secure Base model into the UEA Moving to Adoption model is essential to understanding and supporting the foster carers, the adopters, the professional network, and the child's experiences of their world, in order to contribute to a successful move from foster care to adoption. Many themes described here in relation to attachment theory and the dimensions of the Secure Base model will feature in discussions about different stages of the child's move in subsequent chapters.

For more details of the Secure Base model and practice resources, see https://www.uea.ac.uk/groups-and-centres/centre-for-research-on-children-and-families/secure-base-model.

Chapter 3
Social work practice before the adoption match to support a successful move

INTRODUCTION

This chapter considers social work practice with foster carers and children from the time an adoption plan is made, up to the point where an adoptive family is identified for the child. During this period, foster carers may need skilled support to help them to provide loving, secure base caregiving in their family, while at the same time holding in mind that the child will in due course move to another family. Children of all ages will need a social worker alongside them who is sensitive to their feelings and responses and who can offer support that is adapted to their age and stage of development. There will also be important work with birth relatives to help prepare them for the adoption and their future role for the child.

Skilled and sensitive social work practice at this stage will support the child-focused approach of the UEA Moving to Adoption model, described in Chapters 4, 5 and 6.

SUPPORTING AND PREPARING FOSTER CARERS FOR THE CHILD'S MOVE

Secure base relationships in any type of foster care placement have a therapeutic value for children and young people of all ages. Secure base caregiving is focused on reducing the child's anxiety while promoting their development. When children feel less anxious, they are more able to play, explore, learn and develop. At the same time, they learn to trust that adults will be there to meet their needs, and to experience themselves as loved and loveable.

When there is an adoption plan, it is important that the foster carer is able to provide warm, consistent secure base caregiving, while at the same time finding sensitive and appropriate ways to prepare the child for leaving their family at a later stage. This is a complex process for foster carers, and they will need careful preparation and ongoing support through the practical tasks and the range of emotions involved.

Using the framework of the Secure Base model, the role of the fostering social worker is to support foster carers to build the child's sense of security within each of the five caregiving dimensions of the model, whilst also sowing the seeds for the move to adoption. To facilitate this, the fostering social worker can provide reliable and consistent support, which reduces the foster carer's anxiety and allows them to express and manage the range of their own feelings and to develop their therapeutic role for the child. In this way, the relationship with the social worker can be seen as *providing a secure base for the foster carer.*

For each dimension of the Secure Base model, the key tasks for the foster carer and the fostering social worker are outlined below. This builds on the detailed explanations of the Secure Base dimensions in the previous chapter.

Availability – helping the child to trust

Key tasks for foster carers in preparing the child for the move

Throughout the child's placement in short-term foster care, foster carers should be encouraged and supported to build the child's trust by providing both physical and emotional availability. Children's past experiences will have made it challenging for them to trust caregivers, and this requires focused caregiving strategies for demonstrating availability.

When the plan for adoption is made, the child's need for physical and emotional availability from the foster carers will remain the same, but will evolve in different ways as the foster carers prepare the way for the child's move at a later stage.

For example:

● Foster carers will need to provide all children, from infancy onwards, with focused time and energy during the daily routines of feeding/meal-times, playing, bedtime and waking. Structured routines, verbally scaffolded by the foster carer, will help the child to predict their world and to trust that their needs will be met, both in the present, and by the future adopters.

● Some babies and young toddlers may have established their trust in the foster carers, but be reluctant to trust others to meet their needs, even those in the close foster family circle. Preschool and early school age children may also have continued to be very specific about trusting only in their foster carers. In these cases, the foster carer might plan to support the child to relate comfortably to other familiar adults. Initially, this might be through playing with extended family members, or a baby being offered a favourite food by someone who is a frequent visitor to the household, with the foster carer present at first, then in another room but still available, and so on. Foster carers can think flexibly about creating opportunities for the infant or older child to learn that other familiar adults can be trusted.

- Equally, some children will be indiscriminate in their affections and readily hold up their arms to be held, or approach strangers as if they were trusted adults. For these children, the foster carer will need to ensure that caregiving and cuddles are only given by trusted adults within the household, and that the child is gently guided away from inappropriate connections with others.

- For verbal, older children, who can anticipate (although not fully understand) the prospect of adoption, there will be uncertainty to manage, including when the move might take place, where they might go, or even if an adoptive family will be found at all. The whole team around the child, including the foster carers, will need to plan when and how the plan for adoption is explained to the child, based on the particular needs and circumstances of the individual child.

- Foster carers are key in helping children to manage the inherent uncertainties around an adoption plan at this early stage by offering reassuring predictability in the here and now, while at the same time gently introducing the concept of changes in the future, as appropriate, and acknowledging the inherent difficulties of this for the child.

- It is worth remembering that infants and toddlers may also start to sense change (perhaps in response to new people coming to the house, or foster carers seeming rather preoccupied) without understanding what that change will be. They may react to this with some anxiety, and the caregiver may need to provide additional comfort and nurture to reassure the child that their needs will continue to be met in the foster home.

- Books and stories that depict different family forms can introduce the idea that children's needs for food, care and love can be met in many different types of family (Argent, 2007; Griffiths and Pilgrim, 2007; Merchant, 2010; Robertson, 2018a, b and c). Books may also be used to explore the subject of moving and to explain the process of finding a new family to the child (Kahn, 2003; Daniel, 2009; Argent, 2012).

EXAMPLE

This foster carer is helping a young child to trust and enjoy their place in the foster family, while at the same time introducing the idea of change, accepting that the child may not fully understand this:

We talk a lot about families and she loves naming people in the household, including the pets we have. She knows she is one of our family and we talk about our family being a helping family and that she will move on to her forever family soon – this is a hard concept for her to understand though. We read books and stories about different families to help this process.

In this example, availability and building trust are linked to helping the child understand family membership, a key element of the move.

SUGGESTIONS FOR PRACTICE

Providing availability for the foster carer

- Demonstrate secure base availability to the foster carer by visiting regularly, being available on the phone and responding efficiently to calls and messages, ensuring cover for holidays and absences, building the carer's trust in the availability of help if the process of helping the child move to the adoptive family becomes stressful.

- Keep the foster carer fully informed of all developments in the child's case, including the family-finding process.

- Help the foster carer to understand the reasons for any delay in the progress of the child's plan and help them to manage the strain of this.

Supporting the foster carer to be available to the child and build their trust

- Talk through foster family daily and weekly routines and activities to ensure that there is sufficient caregiving time and energy to focus on the child. Discuss ideas for adjusting family life, or providing additional support if needed to facilitate this.

- Use the 'Availability – helping the child to trust' section of the Secure Base developmental checklist (Appendix 1) to talk about the child's current behaviours in this area and to highlight and develop helpful caregiving approaches. Secure Base positive caregiving approaches (Appendix 2) may be used to develop ideas.

- Help the foster carer to overcome concerns that if the child feels loved and fully included in their foster family, they will find it harder to settle with their adopters. Develop the foster carer's understanding that loving and trusting relationships in foster care help to form a solid foundation for building trust in a new family.

- Discuss the significance of the foster carer's physical and emotional availability before, during and after the moving period. For example, physical availability might include being thoughtful about the timing of family holidays and planning other major commitments around the moving period. Emotional availability might include the timing of additional or further placements, and there might be discussions about the difficulties of supporting a child to settle in to their new family, while at the same time, focusing on the intensive caregiving needed to help a new child to settle in to the foster family.

Sensitivity – helping the child to manage feelings

Key tasks for foster carers in preparing the child for the move

Sensitivity, or the capacity to think about what the child is thinking and feeling, and to reflect that back to the child (and so help them to express and manage their often mixed feelings) is an especially relevant dimension of caregiving in short-term foster care. Children may have experienced difficult feelings in the past, such as fear and anxiety, and they will feel loss and confusion at the separation from their birth family. Foster carers will need to help the child to manage both positive and difficult feelings during the placement, and especially as the plan for adoption develops.

For example:

- Babies and young toddlers as well as older children may notice the emotional climate of the foster home change – perhaps pleasure and relief when suitable adopters are identified, accompanied by sadness or anxiety in different family members as the plan progresses. Children will benefit from having their own mixed feelings named and understood by the calm and reassuring voice of their foster carer – for example, 'It was really nice to hear about your new family, but I think we both felt a bit sad as well when the social worker came to talk about moving to live with them. Let's just have a cuddle together for a while.'

- Older children will understand a little more about the reality of a move and they will experience a range of feelings, including anger, sadness, anxiety, pleasure and excitement. It is important for children to have all of their feelings accepted and validated by their trusted foster carer.

47

When children only wish to express all positive or all negative feelings (for example, 'I don't want to move' or 'I can't wait to move'), it can be helpful for the foster carer to suggest that mixed feelings are to be expected, along with an overall message that there is much to look forward to. Feeling understood in this way will help the child to regulate and manage their feelings and to feel hopeful for the future.

EXAMPLE

The following foster carer understands that her foster child (aged four) has deep feelings of love for her birth mother, and the carer senses that the introduction of a new adoptive mother will need to be managed carefully. The social worker provides a reflective space for the foster carer's concerns (which are based on her sensitivity to the child) to be shared. The outcome is that the foster carer makes a valuable contribution to the moving plan:

My social worker said, 'There's something on your mind, what is it?' and I said, 'Please will you ask if the adoptive mother minds not being called 'Mummy', because this little girl has got her Mummy and Mummy isn't going to change for a long time for her.' And I was glad I'd said it because the adoption worker explained it all to them (the adopters) and she was introduced as 'Mum'. So [the child] was quite happy with that. In her mind, she had Mummy and she had Mum, and they were different people but they both loved her in different ways.

Again, in this example the carer's sensitivity to a child's emotional needs was linked to a family membership message that the child could feel connected and belong to more than one family.

SUGGESTIONS FOR PRACTICE

Providing sensitivity to the foster carer

● Help to prepare foster carers for the range of feelings that they, and other family members, might experience when an adoptive family is identified. This can be done through both training and providing a reflective space in support and supervision visits. Sadness and anxiety about separation from the child are common, even when there may also be pleasure that the child has found a permanent family, and foster carers will need to be reassured that these feelings are understandable and should be expressed and managed in whatever ways they feel are most helpful. The feelings of all foster family members (including both partners, other children in the family, grandparents and others who have had close involvement with the child) should also be considered in this way.

- Reassure foster family members that their feelings of loss and sadness are indicators of how much the child is loved and valued in the foster family, and that this will help the child to trust that they will also be loved and valued in the new family.

- On occasion, the potential loss of the child might trigger memories and feelings around other losses that the foster carer or the family have experienced in the past. The role of the support worker may be critical here in helping caregivers to express and trace the origins of their feelings, listening and responding sensitively. Additional therapeutic support may sometimes be needed if these feelings become overwhelming.

- In some cases, where caring for the child has placed the foster family under strain, there may be feelings of relief that the child will be moving on, and these feelings also need to be acknowledged and validated.

Supporting the foster carer to be sensitive to the child

- Use the 'Sensitivity – helping the child to manage feelings' section of the Secure Base developmental checklist (Appendix 1) to talk about the child's current behaviours in this area and to highlight and develop helpful caregiving approaches. Secure Base positive caregiving approaches (Appendix 2) may be used to develop ideas.

- Help foster carers to understand that children do not always show their feelings directly and consistently. For example, a child might defend themselves against feelings of sadness and anxiety by appearing "fine" and eager to move, or anger might be indicated by the child rejecting or trying to control adults.

- Help foster carers to think about the child's previous experiences of caregiving, separation and loss (when this is complex, the sharing and discussion of a timeline may be helpful) and the ways in which these experiences may affect the ways the child will think and feel about the move to an adoptive family.

Acceptance – building the child's self-esteem

Key tasks for foster carers in preparing the child for the move

Secure base caregiving will address issues of low self-esteem by demonstrating to children of all ages that they are accepted and valued for who they are, praising and celebrating their achievements and also supporting them through disappointments and setbacks.

As the adoption plan develops, the caregiving goal is to ensure that the child's self-esteem is as positive as possible. Messages of being valued and accepted in the foster family may need to become even more clear and explicit, raising the child's confidence and helping them to expect that they will be valued and accepted members of their new family.

For example:

- Some older children develop a belief that they have to leave the foster home because they are "naughty", "difficult", "unloveable" or "not good enough". Foster carers will need to be especially careful to use positive language, showing warmth and affection, using every opportunity to praise the child and demonstrate that they are valued, loved and loveable.

- When talking to older children about their earlier history, foster carers may need to reassure the child that they are not to blame for what has happened in the past, and to explain clearly that the reasons they had to leave the birth family were the responsibility of the adults, not the child. The child's life story book should include a helpful and appropriate way of explaining the reason for the child being in care and placed for adoption that foster carers can draw on to help protect the child's self-esteem.

- All children can be helped to prepare for change in their family environment in the future by a foster family approach that accepts and celebrates differences in ethnicity, sexuality, lifestyles and family norms. This approach can be demonstrated through books, toys, games and food that reflect diversity, and by ensuring that the conversations and language used in the household are respectful and fully accepting of difference.

> **EXAMPLE**
> *We made a special book of photos of all the lovely times we'd had with her as a family. I wanted her always to know how much we loved her and enjoyed having her, and I wrote that in the book, too.*
> (Foster carer)

> **SUGGESTIONS FOR PRACTICE**
>
> *Providing acceptance to the foster carer*
>
> - Aim to establish an accepting and empathic supervisory relationship with the foster carer, building their self-esteem and enabling them to recognise their strengths in caring for the child, and also to receive support when there are difficulties.
>
> - Acknowledge the positive steps that the child is making and the achievements of all foster family members in both accepting and integrating the child into the family and preparing themselves for the child to move.

- Hold in mind that caring for a needy child can have a negative impact on the foster carer's self-esteem, sometimes leading to feelings of being inadequate and unsuited to fostering. In addition, some foster carers have reported that moving the child to another family has created feelings of having failed the child in a fundamental way. Help the foster carer to express and explore these and other difficult feelings and to view them as "understandable in the circumstances". Once distressing emotions are processed in this way, caregivers can gain access to more positive feelings about themselves and the child. They can become less preoccupied by the fear of failure and rejection and be able to think more creatively about their caregiving strategies.

Supporting the foster carer's acceptance of the child

- Use the 'Acceptance – building self-esteem' section of the Secure Base developmental checklist to talk about the child's current behaviours in this area and to highlight and develop helpful caregiving approaches (Appendix 1). Secure Base positive caregiving approaches may be used to develop ideas (Appendix 2).

- Help foster carers to support the child through the family-finding process in ways that are mindful of the child's self-esteem.

Co-operation – helping the child to feel effective

Key tasks for foster carers in preparing the child for the move

Throughout the short-term placement, foster carers should aim to establish a co-operative relationship with the child, negotiating within safe boundaries and helping them to feel a sense of agency and effectiveness. Many children entering care will have lacked the experience of this type of relationship with a caregiver. As a result, they may appear passive and lacking a sense of agency, or attempt to be controlling of adults and peers. A co-operative approach from the foster carers can help the child to feel a sense of agency and effectiveness as they prepare for the changes ahead.

For example:

- Babies and young toddlers will not have developed an understanding of the concept of co-operation ('If we do this now, you can do that later'). Here, the focus needs to be on promoting a sense of agency and choice through gentle caregiving strategies, games and toys that allow the child to make choices, to feel effective and to enjoy working together with the carer. At the same time, it is important to be clear and unequivocal about important boundaries, such as those which are needed to keep the child safe, as these will also need to be set by the adopters later on.

MOVING TO ADOPTION

- For all older, verbal children, discussion of a future move will raise anxieties and for some, there may be difficult memories of previous moves in which they had no preparation or sense of agency. It is important, then, to convey to the child that their views about the planned move are valued and that they will be listened to when decisions are being made about them.

- As appropriate, and guided by the social worker, there should be open and sensitive discussion with the child about the family-finding process and ongoing reassurance that this will include elements of choice for them.

EXAMPLE

This foster carer reflects on the lack of agency that a baby will have experienced during a previous move, the longer-term impact that this has had, and the strategy that she has used to help him to predict his environment and feel more confident and competent as he has grown older.

We've got a little one and when he was brought to us at nine months, he was put into a car at night and he went to sleep and he didn't wake up when we carried him into the house. So when he woke up everything was different and I'm sure he never forgot that. So we've always made a point, even when he was tiny, of explaining everything to him in advance, where we we're going, who would be there, that we'd be back in time for tea. So he expects that now and if you don't [explain in advance] he will get worried and say 'What next? What next?'

SUGGESTIONS FOR PRACTICE

Working co-operatively with the foster carer

- Provide relevant training to ensure that the foster carer feels well prepared and competent to manage the child's move to adoption.

- When a plan for adoption is made, use support and supervision sessions to explain the family-finding and matching process carefully and to recap on the foster carer's role in supporting the child through this process. Update the foster carer regularly on progress, or lack of progress in family-finding.

52

- Hold in mind that the foster carer has key information about the child's preferences, personality, physical and emotional development and how these may have changed during the placement. The significance of this information for the family-finding and matching process should be stressed. Foster carers need to be encouraged and supported both to note and record this information in some detail and then to participate in matching discussions.

- Foster carers will also need to be involved in planning the stages and timeframes involved for supporting the child's move. The principles and approaches from the UEA Moving to Adoption model can be shared with the foster carers. The role of the foster carer through the three stages of the model should be explained.

Supporting the foster carer to work co-operatively with the child

- Use the 'Co-operation – helping the child to feel effective' section of the Secure Base developmental checklist to talk about the child's current behaviours in this area and to highlight and develop helpful caregiving approaches (Appendix 1). Secure Base positive caregiving approaches may be used to develop ideas (Appendix 2).

- Discuss with the foster carer the terms that they and others close to the child will use to help the child to understand the family-finding and matching process. It is important to think about how the child might understand adult terminology, and to ensure that the story about the move that builds in the child's mind is one in which they have a sense of agency and choice.

- When siblings are placed together, support the foster carer to work with each child individually and to hold in mind that they may have very different understandings, hopes and fears about the move. Foster carers may need additional support and specific advice on how to work with siblings who are to be placed separately.

EXAMPLE

A four-year-old was told that his social worker was "looking for a family" for him, as part of engaging him in understanding the adoption process. He later disclosed to his foster carer that he thought the social worker was driving around in her car, looking for a family on the street. He was, understandably, anxious about what sort of family they would be, and that he would have to go and live with them as soon as they had been "found".

> The foster carer and social worker worked together on a child-focused approach to describing the adopter approval and family-finding processes to the child. The child was reassured that he would be safe in his new family, that they would be able to understand and meet his needs, and that his foster carer would explain everything to him along the way.

Family membership – helping the child to belong

Key tasks for foster carers in preparing the child for the move

When foster carers can demonstrate to the child that they are fully welcomed and included in the foster family, the child will gain an important sense of belonging to the family group. At the same time, foster carers must promote a sense of birth family belonging, as appropriate, both through enabling and supporting contact and through sensitive and respectful references to birth family members in the foster home. As the plan for adoption develops, foster carers will need to use care and subtlety to introduce a third element of family membership, giving the message that 'While you are here, you are part of this family' *and* 'One day, you will also be part of a new family'.

For example:

- For babies and toddlers, the concept of being part of the foster family can be promoted from an early stage. The child can be introduced to close and trustworthy family members and given a sense of being welcomed and included in this family group. Family routines and rituals will become familiar and enjoyed and the child will pick up warm, inclusive messages from members of the family group.

- Even when fully verbal, children continue to use non-verbal communication to gain a lot of their clues about the world. For example, they will notice small details of family life which indicate that they are treated in exactly the same way as children born into the foster family and that they are fully included. Similarly, relaxed conversations about different family forms (some families have two daddies or two mummies) or cultures (some families prefer not to eat meat) can help to prepare the child for membership of a different type of family in the future. These conversations can be supported by relevant books, stories, TV programmes and films shared and discussed, as appropriate, with the child.

- For children of all ages, foster carers can prepare special items to support the child's memories and sense of having been a loved and valued member of the foster family. These might include:

  - A book of labelled photos, drawings, tickets, and so on, reflecting the child's stay in the foster family.

- A memory box, containing labelled items that have been significant in the foster home, such as a first pair of shoes, a lock of baby hair, a favourite baby toy, and so on.

- Foster family photos (including pets) that adopters can use to help the child to think and talk about the foster family, and be reassured that foster family members still think and care about them.

- A recording or video message from foster family members, providing individual reflections on the child's stay in the family and/or good wishes for the future.

EXAMPLE

This foster carer describes a visual and very powerful way of demonstrating to each foster child that they are part of the foster family, and introducing the idea of moving to another family in a gentle and reassuring way:

We keep photos of every child we've fostered on our noticeboard, and they all have their story. And she loves to name them all and have me tell her their story – just a simple story like 'She went to live with her special family when she was four and she loves it there, and they love her, and she will live there until she's grown up'.

SUGGESTIONS FOR PRACTICE

Providing a sense of belonging for the foster carer

- Enable the foster carer to feel fully involved as an important member of the team around the child, and to share a joint commitment to the child's successful move to adoption.

- Provide opportunities for the foster carer to take part in training and support groups, or to connect with other foster carers who have helped to move a child to adoption. Some fostering services offer a "buddy" system to link sensitive foster carers who are experienced in moving children with those who are new to the task.

Supporting the foster carer to provide a sense of belonging for the child

- Use the 'Family membership – helping the child to belong' section of the *Secure Base developmental checklist* to talk about the child's current thinking and relationships in the family and to highlight and develop helpful caregiving approaches (Appendix 1). *Secure Base positive caregiving approaches* may be used to develop ideas (Appendix 2).

- Support the foster carer in thinking about how all adult and child members of the foster family feel about this child and the plan for adoption. Identify positive ways in which each can enjoy including the child as a family member while also supporting the move to the new family. This may require being aware of how foster family members handle their feelings of love, loss or possibly relief that the child is moving on.

- Discuss with foster carers the importance of respecting and valuing the child's birth family identity and relationships *and* introducing the idea of the child's future membership of a new adoptive family. Help them to think carefully about the active role that they can take in supporting both sets of relationships appropriately and positively.

- Initiate sensitive discussion around the full range of adoptive family forms, locations and parenting styles that might be appropriate for the child. This can help foster carers to keep an open mind about the type of adoptive family they would like for the child and to avoid disappointment in the future if their sense of what would be ideal is not fulfilled.

SUPPORTING AND PREPARING THE CHILD FOR THE MOVE

When the plan for adoption is confirmed, the child's social worker will need to make an assessment of the child's placement needs, including how best to support the child's move and the adoptive family skills and structure that will best meet the child's needs. This assessment will explore a range of issues, including the child's development, their history of caregiving, losses and change of caregiver, attachment relationships, and their individual personality.

The placement needs of siblings is also a frequently occurring issue for assessment at this stage. The large majority of looked after children in the UK have one or more full or half-siblings or step-siblings, and they typically come from larger groupings of siblings than the general population (Jones and Henderson, 2017). Even when a child has been separated from their sibling(s) or never lived with them, as is the case with many adopted children, an identity as part of a sibling group may remain important and the loss or absence of a sibling may be felt across the lifespan. Beckett (2021) provides comprehensive guidance and signposts helpful resources for assessing the placement needs of siblings.

The assessment of the child's needs should be multi-sourced, and the social worker will need to listen to the foster carer's experiences of caring for the child and to work collaboratively with other professionals who know the child and with birth family members, wherever possible.

At the heart of the assessment, however, is the social worker working directly with the child through play, observation and life story work, where appropriate. Throughout this process, the social worker's thinking and practice can be underpinned by the principles and dimensions of the Secure Base model, as follows.

- **Availability – helping the child to trust**
  The social worker's secure base availability for the child is key, with the social worker relationship helping to reduce the child's anxiety and to build trust in adults. To achieve this, the social worker needs to be accessible to the child through regular visits that the child knows about – for example, the next visit being marked on a calendar that the child can see and understand – or, for older children, through email or messaging. When visits have to be delayed or postponed, the child's trust can be sustained by clear communication and an age-appropriate apology and explanation. The social worker can demonstrate emotional availability through listening carefully and gently reflecting on and putting into words the feelings that the child may be expressing through words or behaviour. As the child's trust in the social worker develops, they will begin to feel safe enough to share important thoughts and feelings about their past, current and future relationships.

- **Sensitivity – helping the child to manage feelings**
  Sensitivity underpins the work necessary to build as accurate a picture as possible of what is in the child's mind – much of which will be inferred rather than directly communicated. Finding age-appropriate approaches to tuning in to the child's world may provide important indicators of their appraisal of past events and moves (e.g. being rescued, taken away or given away). Approaches that are suited to the individual child can be used to help them to develop more accurate understandings of past and future events and to express the range of feelings they may have about them. The social worker can validate the child's feelings and anxieties, whilst also reassuring them that they are understandable and can be managed.

- **Acceptance – building self-esteem**
  Children may have previously experienced caregivers who found it hard to give praise and encouragement. At the same time, when children are moved from their birth families into foster care or begin to think about future separation, it is common for their self-esteem to be diminished, and some may feel a sense of being at fault or responsible for past events or future moves. Social work visits have the potential to build the child's self-esteem by offering consistent interest in the child and showing delight in their achievements and progress. When things have

not gone well, it is equally important to provide signals that the child continues to be accepted and valued for who they are.

- **Co-operation – helping the child to feel effective**
  It is common for children in the care system to report or indicate a lack of agency in their lives – a sense that they do not have a voice, and that others are in control of what happens to them. This can result in the child struggling to be in control, or finding it hard to be appropriately assertive. The social worker can counter these feelings by active attempts to involve the child, as appropriate, in all discussions about their life, including contact with birth relatives, the planning that is taking place, and eventually the move itself. Wherever it is possible for the child to have some choice about what they would like to happen or would prefer not to happen, this is important, although it is equally important that they do not feel the burden of a difficult decision such as the reduction of contact.

- **Family membership – helping the child to belong**
  It is to be hoped that the child will be fully included as a member of the foster family, and the social worker can support this through practical arrangements such as the appropriate delegation of authority to the foster carers.

A sense of belonging in the birth family is equally significant in the early stages of a placement, but the nature of this will shift and change as the adoption plan forms, and sensitive life story work (see below) may be needed to help the child to understand and express their feelings about these changes. Important at this stage is the gathering of information about the birth family, including photos, key dates and addresses, and "soft" information, such as interests and talents. This information should be carefully labelled and stored for use in life story books and later life letters.

As the adoption plan develops, and the idea of a new family membership is introduced, children may need reassurance that it is "OK" to feel a comfortable sense of belonging to more than one family: belonging to a new adoptive family does not have to take away a sense of belonging to the foster family or birth family.

LIFE STORY WORK, LIFE STORY BOOKS AND LATER LIFE LETTERS

Life story work

For children who are to be placed for adoption beyond infancy, social workers or other professionals may need to begin the process of life story work. The aim of life story work is to help the child to develop an age-appropriate and coherent narrative of their lives that can help them to understand and reflect on the journey they have taken, from birth through to joining their adoptive family. Life story work should help the child to think and talk about their story without feeling overwhelmed or having to defend against painful thoughts about the past.

The child's readiness for this work should be carefully assessed in discussion with the foster carer and others close to the child. The work should take place over a number of planned sessions, with the child's responses carefully observed, and the plan adapted if necessary. When the child is part of a sibling group, they may feel more comfortable working together, or some may enjoy individual sessions. Whether or not siblings are seen together, it is important to consider the individual aspects of each child's life story, as well as the experiences they have shared.

It is especially important to help the child to express their own recollections and ideas about their history, as their appraisal of events may be misleading (e.g. 'My parents couldn't look after me because I was too naughty') and so have a negative influence on the child's emotional development in the future. Siblings may understand or remember the same event in different ways. Life story work can address misleading ideas by gently helping the child to gain more accurate understandings (e.g. 'Children are not responsible for adult behaviours and decisions').

If children are to benefit from life story work, they need to feel supported and safe enough to explore difficult feelings and events. This is facilitated by having a trusted person (usually the social worker or a therapist, with the foster carer either present or fully informed of the sessions) alongside them and able to help them to manage their positive and painful feelings. A familiar framework can help children to express and shape their memories and experiences, as this foster carer describes:

> The social worker was amazing. She brought this tree [picture] out each week when she came. She called it the telling tree. And the children would put pictures of the family on the tree, like leaves, and get to talk about how they felt about each member of the family. And she would tell them things as well, and it really helped them process the whole thing. And one of them, she got to find out who her real father was for the first time, in a way that just felt really safe and natural.

An approach to life story work that is informed by the Secure Base model and knowledge of child development can help to shape practice in this area. Seen through this lens, the role of the social worker or therapist in undertaking life story work can be seen as providing a secure base for exploration – in this case, exploration of the past, present and future. If availability, sensitivity, acceptance and co-operation are present in the relationship with the professional, the child is likely to feel safe enough to think about and reflect on the past, and to feel hopeful for the future.

Additionally, however, the child will bring their characteristic strategies for managing stress and anxiety to this relationship and to the painful task of exploring the past. For example:

- The child may be open to a secure, balanced, undefended and straightforward discussion about the past that allows for complexity and difficult feelings ('I know my mother wanted to look after me when she first had me, but she started taking drugs and she didn't look after me properly and then her boyfriend hurt me. That upset me a lot').

- The child may shut down on and deny feelings, dismissing the value of relationships ('I don't mind/don't care about my mum; I don't remember anything').

- The child may be preoccupied and angry about relationships and defensively split them into wholly good and wholly bad ('My mother was the best/worst mother ever and I love her/will never speak to her again).

- The child may have a range of controlling strategies for not engaging with difficult questions ('You can't make me do life story work'; 'I'm not listening').

An awareness of these different strategies and an attunement to the individual child can help to guide the social worker's approach in ways that are sensitive to each child's thinking and feeling. Siblings may have different strategies from each other, even if they have grown up together, and individualised thinking about this will ensure that each child in the sibling group is understood and responded to sensitively.

Life story work is often undertaken before a child moves to adoption, but it can never be isolated as a one-off event. Some types of information about the past can be managed more productively by children at different developmental stages, and all children become better able to think and to allow negative and positive feelings to be expressed and processed once they feel more secure. Life story work, therefore, may need to be revisited in the weeks and months after placement and indeed, adopted children may continue to review the events of their life throughout childhood, adolescence and into adulthood, perhaps at times needing professional input to help them with this.

Life story books

Statutory guidance in England and Wales states that: 'All children with a plan for adoption must have a life story book' (Department for Education (DfE), 2013, p. 107). For older, verbal children, life story books can form a record of the life story work that has been undertaken. For younger, pre-verbal children, the book will be prepared without their direct involvement, but taking careful account of what is important to them. Where appropriate, the book may be accompanied by a memory box, containing carefully labelled objects relevant to the child's early life, such as clothing, baby toys, special gifts, and so on.

The life story book should contain a collection of information, photos and artefacts connected to the child's life gathered from a wide range of sources, including birth family members, foster carers, nurseries, schools, and other agencies or individuals who have played a part in the child's life. Although the book reflects the story of the child's life, the narrative does not have to be linear. Rees (2017), for instance, suggests that the book begins with the child's life as a member of the adoptive family, before looking back to their earlier lives, and then forward to a positive and hopeful future.

Life story books have traditionally focused on the birth family, but it is important that in addition the child's period of time in care, and in particular in the foster family they move from into their adoptive family, is included. Foster carers need to be encouraged to collect photos, mementos of foster family life and birth family contact, and relevant items, such as some of the child's paintings from nursery, from the start of a young child's placement. These help the child's sense of being valued and the sense of continuity of self and identity, whether they are returning home, moving to relatives or joining an adoptive family.

A sensitive but important aspect of the life story book is that it should find ways of addressing difficult events and decisions, which are carefully attuned to the child's age and stage of development. Whilst it is inappropriate to include details that are explicit or distressing, it can also be misleading for the child if difficult life events are avoided or glossed over. Adopted young people themselves have stated that they value simple, factual accounts of their stories, which can be developed over time, as they grow older (Dibben et al, 2018).

Later life letters

The later life letter is also a statutory requirement (DfE, 2013, p. 107), to be written by the child's social worker at the time of the adoption and intended to support the growing understanding of the future adopted adolescent or young adult. This document should provide further factual details about the birth family and the events leading up to the adoption, and should avoid speculation about the motives or decision-making of birth family members.

Each of the social work tasks described above can be underpinned by the principle of respecting the adopted child's identity and relationships. Birth relatives should be consulted and involved as far as possible in each task. Some birth relatives may choose to write their own letter to the child; others may be able to provide photos, information or objects such as birth tags, toys, and so on. The life story book, memory box and later life letter should all be of the highest quality and demonstrate respect for each of the birth family members, professionals and others involved in the story. Each item will contribute to the growing child's sense of self and identity and, as well as tackling difficult issues, as described above, each should contain positive messages about the child's history, birth family members and community.

There are a number of very helpful practice guides and training sessions on communicating with children, undertaking life story work, ascertaining children's wishes and feelings, compiling life story books and writing later life letters. (For example, see Fahlberg, 1994; Camis, 2001; Shah and Argent, 2006; Gilligan, 2009; Corrigan and Moore, 2011; Maye, 2011; Ryan and Walker, 2016; Hammond and Cooper, 2013; Rees, 2017; Moffatt, 2020.) The needs of sibling groups are specifically addressed in Beckett (2021).

The Siblings' Charter

Although the majority of siblings who have grown up together are placed for adoption together, there are also those for whom placement together is assessed to be unhelpful or too difficult to achieve. Additionally, there are many children who may be placed for adoption with at least one full, half or step-sibling living elsewhere.

In the majority of cases, therefore, life story work and life story books and letters will need to address the issue of siblings in some way. The Siblings Charter (Beckett, 2021) provides a helpful checklist for a quality service:

- I know the reasons why I am not living with all my brothers and sisters.

- I have information and explanations in my life story book about my brothers and sisters.

- I have met the family who care for my brothers and sisters.

- I know that my family met my brothers and sisters and have photos of us all together.

- I receive news about my brothers and sisters and how they are doing.

- I have recent photos of my brothers and sisters.

- I know when I will see my brothers and sisters (or why I cannot see them).

- I know that I can talk about and ask questions about my brothers and sisters.

FAMILY-FINDING

A range of approaches may need to be used to find an appropriate family for some children, especially those who are older and in sibling groups. It is important to note that these activities should be distinct from, and in addition to, the planned contacts and meetings that are recommended in Stage 1 of the UEA Moving to Adoption model.

Two common family-finding approaches are highlighted here:

- A "one-off" meeting between the adopters and the child may be used to help the prospective adopters to come to a decision about whether or not this is the right child for them, and therefore whether or not they would like to proceed with the match. These meetings are sometimes called pre-meets, chemistry meets, or mini-meets.

- Adoption activity days (AADs) are now an established area of practice and serve a similar purpose to one-off meetings. They have been helpful in finding families for some children, especially those with additional needs. There is helpful practice guidance available on running AADs (Fursland and Betts, 2015), much of which is also applicable to one-off meetings.

A key issue for these approaches is that of preparing and informing the child. There has been discussion in the sector about the level of openness that is manageable for children. There have been concerns for children who understand the nature of the meeting, and then learn that the adopters did not wish to proceed. In these cases, there is understandable reluctance to take the risk of the child feeling rejected or unwanted. As a result, the practice of "blind viewings" (in which the child is unaware that they are being observed) or "bump intos" (a meeting between the foster carers and the adopters in which the child is present but unaware of the purpose) has developed in some agencies. CoramBAAF (2017) makes clear recommendations for this area of practice, suggesting that all children who are of an appropriate age and understanding should be engaged in their family-finding and therefore sensitively informed and prepared and supported throughout this period. This approach reflects the principles of openness and consultation that should underpin all social work with children.

Children who are properly informed will benefit from a sense that they have some agency and an active engagement in their family-finding. Those who ask further questions about their family-finding process later on can receive honest answers that will fit with their memories and understanding. Adopters who proceed with the match will feel able to talk openly with their child about the process of meeting and getting to know them.

PLANNING BIRTH FAMILY CONTACT

From the child's first entry into care, decision-making about planning and supporting birth family contact is a key area of social work practice, initially working to the possibility of the child returning to live within the birth family. If a plan for adoption is made, the focus changes, since the child's relationships with the birth family will be legally terminated and the child will become a permanent member of a new adoptive family. Nevertheless, the birth family will remain part of the child's history and identity, and individual birth family members may be able to offer important relationships, information and support for the child at different stages of the adoption. With this in mind, contact plans should be made on a case-by-case basis, always underpinned by the principle of respecting and valuing the child's birth family identity and relationships (Neil and Beek, 2020).

Initial meeting between birth relatives and adopters

A "one-off" meeting between the birth parents or other significant relatives and the adopters before the child is placed for adoption is traditionally facilitated wherever possible and can fulfill a range of purposes, including:

- providing adopters with a fuller understanding and greater respect for the birth parents/relatives;

- providing birth parents/relatives with reassurance that their child will be well cared for in the adoptive family;

- providing the child with the reassurance, later on, that their birth parents and adopters have met, and so facilitating further curiosity and questions.

In order to fulfil these purposes, the meetings need to have some degree of structure. For example, adopters may wish to prepare a list of "messages" that they would wish to convey to the birth relative (Sydney and Price, 2014). Birth relatives may also benefit from talking through the questions they would want to ask or the messages they would want to give to the adopters. However, Neil (2010) found that these meetings were less valued by birth parents when they were too tightly controlled, for example, when the birth relative was told not to ask any questions about the adopters' lives. Inevitably, these meetings will be emotional and painful at times, and all parties will need sensitive practical and emotional support afterwards.

These meetings, however, do not have to be "one-offs", and some flexibility might be beneficial. In some cases, for example, it might be agreed that a further meeting after the child is placed would be a positive step. In cases where ongoing direct contact is planned, a series of meetings between the adopters and the birth relative can be used to form a foundation for ongoing contact after the child's placement. This process is important as a way of building trust, talking through the hopes and expectations of the contact and outlining boundaries, as appropriate.

Post-adoption contact

Traditionally, adoption has usually involved a plan for indirect contact only, with direct contact rarely considered. However, there is evidence that indirect arrangements seldom continue for long after the adoption, or even get started in the first place. At the same time, the possibility of positive face-to-face arrangements (especially with supportive extended family members and siblings) is often overlooked (Neil, 2010).

There is now a body of research that has considered the benefits and risks of direct contact. Iyer *et al* (2020) review what is known about the implications of contact for the well-being of children and young people, drawn from 49 studies (conducted over a 20-year period) of children who had been separated from their birth parents in public law contexts. Overall, these studies suggest that well-facilitated contact is associated with children's well-being, both in the short and longer term.

Reflecting on this data, the authors suggest that contact planning should move away from the questions of whether or not there should be contact/how often the contact should be. Instead, a more helpful approach might be to ask: 'How best to facilitate positive experiences and the meaningful involvement of those who matter to the child' (p. 2).

A first step towards preparing for positive contact arrangements of all kinds is the building of trusting and collaborative relationships between birth family members and professionals, since these can form a foundation for a positive contact plan to be developed and for future trust to develop between the birth family member and the adopters. In some cases, the foster carer may also have a role in building these bridges, as this foster mother, who sat in on her foster child's contact visits, describes:

> *I got to know* [birth mother] *really well during those visits, just from watching and listening, and I got quite fond of her and I realised that she didn't pose any threat. She would never harm* [child] *or his adoptive family and she just wanted the best for him. And I tried to convey that to the adopters when the time came.*

When planning contact, the full range of the child's birth family relationships (including both parents, siblings, grandparents, aunts and uncles, cousins, etc) should be considered. Plans should be individualised, with a focus on the benefits that connection with a particular birth family member is likely to have for the child, both in the short, medium and longer term, and how best to shape the contact plan to achieve these benefits.

The factors that facilitate good quality contact are:

- *An approach that takes account of the views and wishes of children.*

- *An approach that recognises the complexities of family and friendship relationships.*

- *Clarity about the purpose of contact among all of those involved.*

- *An approach that is tailored to the needs of each individual child, is flexible, is not formulaic and that takes account of changing circumstances and relationships over time.*

- *An appropriate level of support provided for the child, the carers and the family members or friends involved in contact.*

(Ryan, 2020)

Helpful practice resources for planning contact can be found at: https://contact.rip.org.uk/.

Supporting children during final contacts

In a small number of cases, it might be felt that there are clear risks for the adoptive family if a particular close relative was to have contact after adoption. It may be, then, that a final contact session will be planned. These are sometimes referred to as "Goodbye" or "Goodbye for now" or "Wishing you well" contacts.

Inevitably, these occasions will be difficult for all concerned. For birth relatives, the burden of grief and loss can be immense, as described by this birth mother:

> It was, like, someone taking something away from you, and then falling into a hole. We actually went to a centre room, we had two hours with my daughter and then I had to put my daughter in the car. I think the hardest point was actually putting my daughter in the car and saying goodbye to her and that was the last time I ever saw her face. I think that must have been the hardest time.

Children of all ages will also find these meetings difficult. They are likely to feel very different to previous contact meetings. Babies and toddlers can be unsettled by the strong emotions of the occasion (as described above) and yet they do not have the capacity to understand and make sense of what is happening. Older children will have some understanding that this is a way of saying "Goodbye" and will have their own difficult feelings about this, as well as witnessing the distress of their birth relatives.

Children will need ongoing support to process their feelings after the final contact. The emotional impact of the meeting will be present for some time, even for small babies, and all children may need additional comfort and reassurance to settle back into their normal routines. Older children will need time to think and talk about the contact, while being supported by their foster carers and a trusted social worker. Ideally, there will be sufficient time for these conversations to begin before all are diverted by the emotional demands of meeting with prospective adopters.

Whatever the timing of the reduction in contact or the final contact, there are complex and sometimes conflicting emotional challenges for children at this time. They will need help to process and manage their feelings about their birth family *and* their feelings about leaving the foster family, as well as a combination of anxiety and interest in joining a new family. For the social worker, the task is to hold in mind that the child may need to move between these sets of feelings and be helped to make sense of them and manage them. The team around the child, including the foster carers and the prospective adopters, can be helped to understand and respond sensitively to the complexity of the child's feelings at this time.

EXAMPLES
Providing a secure base for final contacts

Where safe and possible, the secure base availability of the foster carer can help to reassure the child, through the range of situations that can arise before, during and after the final contact. For example:

- A foster carer was able to support the child emotionally and instigate an alternative enjoyable activity when a birth parent could not manage to attend the contact.

- A foster carer described a birth mother becoming distressed, as the baby was fretful when she held him. The foster carer, who already had a positive relationship with the birth mother, was able to step in to calm the baby, model this for the birth mother, then pass the baby back to the birth mother who was then able to have more rewarding interactions with him.

- A foster carer who had been present during the final contact was able to talk with the child afterwards about the games that the birth parents had played with her, and to record this information in her life story book.

68

CONCLUSION

The areas of preparatory work with the child, the foster carers and the adopters outlined above will contribute to a sense of readiness and preparedness for planning the move. When prospective adopters are identified and a match is agreed, a new set of events will be set in train, and it is at this point that the UEA Moving to Adoption model can be used as a framework for practice, as described in the three following chapters.

AN INTRODUCTION TO THE UEA MOVING TO ADOPTION MODEL

The UEA Moving to Adoption model covers the period from the match between the adopters and the child being identified, through to about four weeks after the child is placed for adoption. The model focuses on social work practice with the foster carers, the adopters and the child.

Social work practice with birth relatives during this period is not covered by the model, as this will vary considerably according to the relationships that the child has with the birth relatives and the ongoing contact that is planned, and they will probably not be directly involved in managing the move. However, in all cases, it is important that the child's significant birth relatives are kept informed of the moving plan and the progress of the move, and that future contact plans have been shared with them in draft form, subject to confirmation after the move has been made.

The UEA Moving to Adoption model outlines three key stages of the move, as follows:

- **Stage 1: Getting to know each other**

- **Stage 2: Making the move**

- **Stage 3: Supporting relationships after the move**

The UEA model is not prescriptive about timescales or the details of planning for the child's move. Rather, it suggests some key principles that should be held in mind and applied flexibly according to individual needs and the particular circumstances of each move. Each move should place the child's emotional needs at the centre, while also supporting the foster carers and adopters.

Although the term "child" is generally used throughout the UEA model, it is recognised that some children are moving to adoption as part of a sibling pair or group, and their needs as individuals, as well as their interactions with each other, will need to be taken into account. Some children will have siblings living elsewhere, or occasionally they will be separated from siblings with whom they have previously been living. Each of these moves requires individualised and sensitive planning to ensure that the sibling relationships and identities are respected and sustained in the best possible ways. Beckett (2021) provides helpful guidance for supporting the moves of sibling groups, whether they are to be living together or apart.

It is recognised that there are regional variations in adoption policy and procedures for planning and supporting the move to adoption, across the four UK countries. In addition, there is different legislation and guidance governing adoptions within the UK. However, it is important to note that the key principles of the UEA model are not tied to particular legal or procedural systems and can be applied within each of these variations.

Key principles of the UEA Moving to Adoption model

- Opportunities for the foster carers and adopters to build a positive relationship should be promoted at an early stage in the moving process, as this is helpful to the success of the move.

- The child and the adopters should be given opportunities to become familiar with each other through play and observation prior to the adopters undertaking any caregiving tasks.

- All arrangements and timescales should focus on the needs of the child.

- The child's feelings about the move should be held in mind and responded to sensitively.

- Some continuity of foster family relationships and environment will support the child in managing the loss of the foster family and building trust in the adoptive family.

- There should be flexibility in the planning, in consultation with the child, the families and the social workers, to allow for emerging circumstances and needs.

Each stage of the UEA Moving to Adoption model is underpinned by the five dimensions of the Secure Base model:

- **Availability – helping the child to trust**
  At each stage of the move, the child needs to be able to *trust* that a familiar adult is *physically and emotionally available* to them. Initially, the trusted adult will be the foster carer. Gradually, the child will build trust in the adopters, but will continue to need reassurance and some availability from the foster carer after the move has been made.

- **Sensitivity – helping the child to manage feelings**
  The child may experience a wide range of positive and difficult feelings at each stage of the move. They may need support to manage these feelings. Professionals, foster carers and adopters can help the child by being *sensitive* to their feelings, putting them into words and giving reassurance that they are understandable, and can be managed.

- **Acceptance – building self-esteem**
  At each stage of the child's move, care needs to be taken to ensure that the child's *self-esteem* remains positive. The foster carer can give the child clear messages that they have been loved and *accepted* for who they are in the foster family, and the adopters can reassure the child that this will also be the case in the adoptive family. All games, toys and activities during the moving period should promote self-esteem by being achievable and enjoyable for the child.

- **Co-operation – helping the child to feel effective**
  The child needs to have appropriate choices about aspects of the move, and a sense of *being effective* and involved in the planning. Even very young children can benefit from being helped to understand and anticipate what is going to happen for them at each stage.

- **Family membership – helping the child to belong**
  Through the three stages of the move, the child needs to feel valued and included as part of the foster family, while at the same time being helped to build a *sense of belonging* in the adoptive family.

The three stages of the UEA Moving to Adoption model and the principles that guide them are explored in the next three chapters. Each stage is examined in terms of its aims and objectives, the events that may occur within it and the roles of the professionals involved. Each of the three stages are illustrated by practice examples from a range of sources, including a foster carer diary.

CHAPTER 4
Stage 1: Getting to know each other

INTRODUCTION

Stage 1 of the UEA model begins *after* the match between the adopters and the child has been identified. The aim of Stage 1 is to prepare for the intense period in which the child makes the move to the adoptive home (Stage 2). Stage 1 involves a gradual process of familiarisation in which the foster carers and the adopters, and similarly, the adopters and the child, can get to know each other and begin to build trust, *without the adopters taking on caregiving tasks for the child.*

During this period, the foster carers can develop confidence in the adopters' capacity to understand, love and care for the child. Adopters can observe the relationship between the child and the foster carers and build their trust in the foster carer's capacity to support the child through the move. When the child becomes involved in the meetings, they will see that their trusted foster carer is comfortable in the presence of the adopters and so feel more able to take the risk of building trust in their new parents.

There is regional variation in the number of contacts between the child and the adopters that take place before the match is taken to the adoption panel, and this should be negotiated locally. However, adoption panels in England are increasingly supportive of (or expect) at least one face-to-face meeting to have occurred before they consider the match (CoramBAAF, 2017).

The use of "chemistry" or "bump-into" meetings has also been developing in Scotland, with the purpose of informing the match with prospective adopters. In Scotland, however, due to the role of the Children's Hearing in the decision about the child's move, observation and play visits between the child and adopters should not take place until the Hearing has agreed the child's change of address, as it is important not to pre-empt the decision of the Hearing. However, the relationship-building between *foster carers and prospective adopters* can start once the match is agreed, and information about the progress of these meetings or contacts should be included in the report submitted by the social worker. The aim of this is to help inform the Hearing about the plan, without pre-empting any decision they might make.[4]

In cases where adopters have had opportunities to meet or play with the child, in order for them to come to a decision about whether or not this is a child whom they might be able to consider as a match, these meetings should not be "counted" as part of the moving process. If a match does proceed in these cases, it is still important that the Stage 1 activities take place, as described below, in preparation for the move. The reason for this is that once the decision to proceed with the match is made, both the adopters' and the foster carers' mindsets will be different; they will be thinking and feeling about the child as the future child of the adoptive family, with all the accompanying changes that will occur in their relationships with each other and with the child.

Key principles at Stage 1

- Opportunities for the foster carers and adopters to build a positive relationship should be promoted at an early stage in the moving process, as this is helpful to the success of the move.

- The child and the adopters should be given opportunities to become familiar with each other through play and observation prior to the adopters undertaking any caregiving tasks.

STAGE 1: GETTING TO KNOW EACH OTHER

What happens in Stage 1?

Meetings between the foster carers and adopters, without the child present

- Stage 1 should begin with some face-to-face contact between the foster carers and the adopters, providing opportunities to get to know each other as adults and to begin the process of working together to support the child through the move.

- As the foster carers and adopters begin to establish a trusting relationship, their anxiety will be reduced and they will become more able to focus on the emotional needs of the child. This will be of benefit to the child at the point when they become involved in the meetings.

---

4   See Appendix 3 for further guidance on professional practice in Scotland.

They will see that their foster carer trusts the adopters and so feel more willing to begin the process of building trust in their new parents. As this adopter put it:

> *I feel that we were given the chance to develop a good relationship with the foster family which, in the end, helped our child feel more comfortable with us.*

- The Secure Base developmental checklist (see Appendix 1) may be completed by the foster carer as appropriate for the age of the child (with or without the social worker) and shared with the adopters at this stage. This can provide a focus for discussion of attachment-related behaviours and positive caregiving responses.

- In all cases, it would be expected that there would be a detailed discussion about the child, in which the foster carer would share their experiences of caring for the child, the child's likes and dislikes, and how best to support their emotional and physical well-being – and for the adopters to respond and ask any questions that they may have.

- The nature and frequency of the meetings and visits will be necessarily diverse, depending on the range of personalities and circumstances involved. The following examples represent these variations:

  - Foster carer and adopter meet for coffee on two occasions, while the child is at nursery.

  - Foster carers and adopters meet on neutral ground on two occasions during the evening.

  - Foster carers and adopters meet once in the foster home, while the child is at school.

  - Phone conversations and exchange of emails, photos, messages or videos may take place between any of these meetings.

- For the majority of foster carers and adopters in the UEA Moving to Adoption pilot study, these adult meetings were successful and valued by all concerned, and warm relationships developed easily, as this adopter describes:

> *We got to know them* [the foster carers] *well before we even met our son. They were supportive, intuitive, understanding and amazing.*

- In a small number of cases in the pilot study, foster carers or adopters indicated a degree of impatience and eagerness for the next steps of meeting the child to take place. The risk here is that the (understandable) desire for forward momentum results in less attention being paid to the child's needs and feelings. Training and support is key in helping foster carers and adopters to understand the value of getting to know each other at this early stage in the moving process and to see it as positive preparation for making the move.

Observe and play sessions

- Observe and play sessions involve the prospective adopters having planned contact with the child, with the foster carer present. The adopters and the foster carers must be carefully prepared for these sessions. They should be advised that during the sessions, the adopters should avoid caregiving tasks. Instead, they should take a back seat and observe the child interacting, as normal, in the foster family. In addition, they may play with the child (if the child initiates this/is comfortable with it), watch television with the child, read stories or share simple local outings with the child and foster carer. The benefits of this approach may be seen later in the process, as this adoptive father notes:

    His trust was helped by playing games with us, and so on for several visits – so we established an element of fun first, then moved on to carer duties.

- It should be explained to both parties that throughout the observe and play session, the foster carer will take the caregiving role and act as a secure base for the child. For example, if the child falls over, the foster carer will offer comfort and reassurance and settle them. This helps to minimise the child's anxiety, allowing them to become familiar and comfortable with the adopters, before taking the next step of trusting them to care for him or her.

- Observe and play sessions will vary in number, frequency and quantity, depending on factors such as the child's age, anxiety level and geographical considerations. Examples from the UEA Moving to Adoption pilot study include:

    - Adopters make five visits to the foster home over eight weeks (child aged four-and-a-half).

    - Adopters make two visits plus e-communication over one week (child aged nine months).

    - Adopters share a series of four family outings with the foster family (child aged two years).

- Ideally, observe and play sessions build on the trusting relationships already established between the foster carers and adopters, and can have the additional benefit of conveying this trust to the child. When the child is able to pick up signals that the adults value and trust each other, they will feel a greater sense of safety in building trust themselves, as noted by this adoptive mother:

    Each time, when we arrived, the foster carer made a point of giving us big hugs in front of our son, so he would know she thought we were OK.

- Occasionally, foster carers or adopters might feel impatient for "hands on" caregiving to start sooner than planned, or the child themself might ask for the adopters to be more involved. In these cases there may need to be some flexibility, with adopters taking on some caregiving tasks (for example, helping the child to put shoes on before an outing) but with the foster carer continuing to take the lead in the primary caregiving tasks such as feeding and nappy changing. The aim is for the child to build trust and feel comfortable with the adopters before taking the next step of trusting them to care for him or her.

- An adoption social worker reflected on the importance of observe and play opportunities, as follows:

  I think what was particularly helpful [in making a positive move] *was the first meetings between children and adopters, with no pressure on the adopters to do any caring tasks and for the children to develop a playful relationship first with them.*

The following adopter of a second child found the Stage 1 visits particularly valuable in terms of helping the whole family to prepare for the arrival of the new child:

The initial meetings with the child help you to really plan for that particular child and what the reality may look like. It gives you plenty of time to adjust to the thought that this child will join your family. It helped us to prepare [birth child] *and it was reassuring to us that they could play well and we could see how the dynamics would change in our family.*

EXAMPLE
Observe and play visits for Toby (nine months)

Toby had been in foster care for six months. He had recently developed a selective attachment to his foster carers and was reluctant to accept care from anyone else, even familiar adults. His foster carer and social worker felt that he would need additional time to become familiar with his prospective adopter before they began caregiving tasks for him. Following contacts between the foster carer and the adopter, a series of Stage 1 observe and play visits were planned, over five consecutive days, as follows:

Day 1 The adopter visits the foster carer for coffee, just before Toby's morning sleep.

Day 2 The adopter spends a morning with the foster carer and Toby, observing all of the foster carer's caregiving tasks and play activities.

Day 3 The adopter spends an afternoon with the foster carer and Toby, observing all of the foster carer's caregiving tasks and joining in some play activities.

Day 4 The adopter spends a morning with Toby, taking a lead in play activities.

Day 5 The adopter spends an afternoon with Toby, playing and accompanying the foster carer to the park where they both play with Toby on the swings and in the sand pit.

These daily visits helped Toby to become familiar with the adopter and to see them as a person whom he could trust enough to engage and have fun with. They also enabled the adopter to feel confident in taking the next steps of caregiving tasks for Toby.

EXAMPLE

Observe and play visits for Alfie (five years)

Alfie had a history of several moves and changes of caregiver. A previous adoption placement disrupted after three months. Alfie was moved to a new foster home where he settled well. After nine months, new prospective adopters were identified.

Alfie was well prepared for his new family by his social worker and foster carer. They worked together, showing him photos of the home and family, giving him simple information and answering his questions. He said that he was worried because he didn't know the adopters and he didn't know what his bedroom would be like. He was reassured when he was told that his foster carers would get to know them first and then he would get to know them a bit at a time, while still living with his foster family, and that he would visit the house and his bedroom with his foster carer before he moved.

The observe and play sessions plan spanned Christmas and covered 30 days, as follows:

Day 1 Adopters visit foster home (one hour).

Day 2 Adopters attend Alfie's fifth birthday celebration at a local park.

Day 4 Adopters visit foster home after school, to observe and play (two hours).

Day 6 Adopters visit foster home after school, to observe and play (two hours).

Day 7 Adopters send card to Alfie.

Day 9 Foster carer takes Alfie to adopters' home for lunch.

Day 11 Adopters visit foster home after school, to observe and play (two hours).

Day 12   Adopters visit foster home after school, to observe and play (two hours).

Day 13   Adopters attend Alfie's school play with foster carers.

Day 15   Adopters visit after school and take Alfie out to tea, with foster carer.

Day 19   Adopters attend school assembly and 'Goodbye from class and teacher' ritual with foster carers.

Day 22   Adopters visit for afternoon (observe and play).

Day 23   Christmas Eve – adopters visit in the morning and visit local park with Alfie.

Day 24   Christmas Day – Facetime call.

Day 25   Boxing Day – Facetime call.

Day 28   Adopters visit foster home 10am–4pm. Play, make lunch for Alfie and foster carer.

Day 30   Local trip out, without foster carer.

- These observe and play sessions enabled Alfie to become very familiar with the adopters and to feel confident and happy that they would become his parents.

- The visit to the adopters' home after the first week of contacts was effective in reducing Alfie's anxiety. After the visit, he frequently referred to his new bedroom, the family cat and other elements of the house, and he was able to ask more questions and begin to anticipate the reality of the move.

- The schedule enabled the adopters to be present for key events in his life (his birthday, the school play) and to be part of the process of letting go of his life in the foster home (attending the school farewell assembly).

- Some sessions involved the foster carers and the adopters sharing enjoyable activities (the school play, a restaurant meal), conveying a shared commitment to and interest in Alfie and his well-being.

- The schedule included face-to-face contacts but also contact when apart (the adopters sent a card when there was a gap in the visits, Facetime calls were made) – demonstrating that the adopters were continuing to hold Alfie in mind even when he could not see them.

> **EXAMPLE**
> **Lucy's move to adoption at 12 months old: a foster carer's diary**[5]
>
> Today we had the second observe and play visit. Lucy's adopters visited for two-and-a-half hours and it was a very relaxed, easy visit. They are so aware of not overpowering her, moving things along at her pace and giving her plenty of space. Considering it is nearly three weeks since she saw them, there was definitely a questioning look about her – a slight spark of recognition. It was definitely helped by using photos of the adopters in the run-up to the visit. I had asked them to laminate A4-sized head and shoulders photos of themselves, which I began using with her on Wednesday. She can hold them, chew them, play with them during the day, and then I attach them to her cot bars so we can say goodnight to Mummy and Daddy, and they will be the first thing she sees in the morning when she wakes.

Preparing for significant changes and some continuity in the new family

- Stage 1 can also provide opportunities for foster carers and adopters, with the support of their social workers, to identify significant changes the child will encounter in the new family, while building in some opportunities for continuity. Examples of practical adjustments that could be made in either family to achieve continuity of the child's environment are as follows:

  - The adopters install a low light/nightlight on the landing, if this is familiar to the child.

  - A child in a pet-free foster home is familiarised with larger dogs, as there is one of these in the new family.

  - There is discussion of familiar items that the foster carer will send with the child (e.g. cutlery, dishes, cups), so that the adopters are aware of this in advance.

  - A foster carer uses the adopters' suggestions and recipes to prepare different foods that the child will encounter in the adoptive family – and vice versa.

---

5   A foster carer who participated in the UEA pilot study kept a detailed diary, charting her foster child's move to adoption. Excerpts from the anonymised diary are used to illustrate key events before, during and after the move, from the foster carer's perspective.

> **EXAMPLE**
> **Lucy's move to adoption at 12 months old: a foster carer's diary**
>
> Together we are thinking about minimising the number of things that will change when Lucy moves. We've agreed that the adopters will borrow our car seat for a few weeks, for several reasons – Lucy isn't quite big enough for the next-sized seat and it would be a waste of money for them to be buying two in such a short time; she is happy and comfortable in the car seat we have and it will keep that familiarity; and it fits on the buggy they have bought. Because I will be visiting for a while after her move, they can let me have it when they've finished with it.

Using virtual contacts alongside Stage 1 visits

Face-to-face contact during Stage 1 can be enhanced and complemented by a wide range of virtual contacts, each contributing to the process in which the foster carers and the adopters, and similarly, the adopters and the child, can get to know each other and begin to build trust.

Virtual communication can be used flexibly, and creative ideas are likely to develop in individual cases. It is helpful to plan the virtual contacts around the same structure as the face-to-face meetings: that is, the adults have the virtual communication without the child present first, then the adopters and the child interact virtually with each other, with the child continuing to be supported by the foster carer as a secure base. This will ensure that overall, the plan remains coherent and the process of building trust in the adopters remains gradual and incremental for the child.

Building the relationship between the foster carers and adopters

- The multiple forms of "virtual" contact (email, phone calls, video calls, messaging) can allow additional conversations between the foster carers and adopters to enable them to get to know each other, become familiar with each other's homes and share information about the child.

- In some cases, it might be necessary to plan for additional members of the foster or adoptive family (such as siblings) to be included at specific times, or for particular issues (such as the management of a child's health condition) to be discussed.

- Foster carers could complete the Secure Base developmental checklist appropriate for the child's age (see Appendix 1) and email a copy to the adopters. They could then have a phone or video call to talk through the completed checklist.

- Adopters and foster carers can work together to plan ways of familiarising the child with the adopters, for example, through the foster carers introducing the child to the adopters' family book, photos and any transitional objects.

Building familiarity between the child and adopters through play and observation

- Virtual communication can provide opportunities for the adopters to "meet" and observe the child both at play and when being cared for by the foster carers. Observation through the camera while the child walks around their toys or bedroom or has a meal is a powerful aid to understanding both the child's development and experience and the foster carer's caregiving style and responses to the child.

- Video (live or recorded) can be used to allow adopters to build familiarity with the child's home environment, routines, likes and dislikes, personality and ways of coping with situations. Also, observing how foster carers manage children's feelings and behaviours is likely to be helpful to adopters, so they can achieve consistency for the child. If these observations are recorded, the adopters (perhaps with their social worker) can reflect on what has been observed, watch and listen for small clues about what the child finds helpful.

- Initial relationships built between the foster carers and adopters will help them to work together to plan the child's inclusion in the contact. During the periods of virtual interactions, the adopters and carers should have time set aside to speak with each other, without the child being involved in the call. They should also plan time to talk individually with their own supporting social workers.

- Foster carers can pass on information to the adopters to help make the virtual contact meaningful and comfortable for the child. This might include the child's likely attention span, ideas about what the child might be interested in, the times of day at which they are more relaxed and ready to interact, questions the adopters could ask, focused on recent events, etc. They can pass information to the adopters, such as the child's favourite songs, stories or hobbies, to allow them to build these into their calls.

- Foster carers should give the child clear messages that they support and trust the adopters by using a warm tone of voice and positive language when introducing calls.

- Foster carers need to remain physically and psychologically available to the child during video calls, for example, with a very young child, sitting the child in their lap while looking at a video. For some older children, it may be possible for foster carers to gradually withdraw/sit back for part of the call, so that the child and adopters can spend time together. However, at this stage, the foster carer is the secure base for the child, so should remain available and rejoin the call if and when the child needs support.

- The foster carer can unobtrusively place the camera or laptop on a table in the foster home and leave it to record or stream the child's daily life. This can allow the adopters to pick up rich detail of daily events and interactions. The adopters could see almost the whole of the child's daily routine over video call, split over a few days.

- From time to time, the adopters could be involved in the routine, for example, calling first thing so they could say 'hello' to the child as they wake up.

- Foster carers can film behaviour that might not be otherwise easily observable, for example, disturbed sleep patterns at night, or tantrums.

- "Smart" video calling tools (e.g. Facebook's "video portal") can allow more of a room to be seen and/or allow adopters to follow the "live" action.

Supporting virtual observation sessions

- Adopters may need to be supported with their expectations of the video calls. It is important to let adopters know that it is OK for children to dip in and out of video calls, and that if a young child can only manage a short time, this is not a rejection or a sign they are doing something wrong. It may be helpful to put a time limit on these "play" interactions of around 20–30 minutes. Foster carers recording the child's reaction to seeing the adopter's videos can be helpful in encouraging the adopters during this period.

- Foster carers and adopters may need practical or financial support with managing video technology.

> **Suggestions for activities that can be planned by foster carers and adopters and shared virtually by both families**
>
> - Undertake the same craft activity, or bake together.
>
> - Read a story over a video call with both the foster carers and adopters having the same book, so that the child can turn the page.
>
> - Eat together, perhaps with the child pretending to "feed" the adopters snacks.
>
> - Adopters could organise a "treasure hunt" or "find the teddy bear game", which can work as a way for the child to learn about their new home. For the hunt to work well, adopters and foster carers may need to plan this together beforehand so the foster carers can suggest places the child might look.

- For an older child, there could be a simple quiz on a subject they are interested in (for example, dogs, trains, dinosaurs), with a few questions each day.

- The families could sing songs or nursey rhymes together.

- The families could play Peek-a-boo or I-spy.

- Video calls can be used in conjunction with communicating by post. For example, adopters could open and look at a child's drawing, posted to them by the foster carer with the child's involvement.

- Suggest playful activities that both foster carers and adopters can use with the child.

- Where there are children already in the adoptive family, consider how they can "meet" and "play" with their new brother or sister virtually. Plan ahead how this will be managed, for example, agreeing for each call who will be involved and for how long.

- For children who have sensory disability, focus on materials and activities that are most appropriate for them – such as using sounds, smells or touching objects for a child with a visual disability, rather than relying on visual cues.

- For young babies (under one year), it is helpful for them to see their adopters' faces and hear their voices so that some familiarity can develop. Adopters responding gently to the child's activities, whether at play or mealtimes, can help the child to experience the adopters as warmly responsive, sensitive to their moods and interested in them – and build attuned, mutually rewarding conversational patterns.

- Adopters could prepare videos for the child to look at with their foster carers at other times of day. For example, reading a story, filmed with the camera over their shoulder looking at the book in their hands, as if the child was sitting in their lap.

- Use video to introduce other children, or the family pets.

- Arrange separate calls for each child in a sibling group if it is difficult for them to share attention on a screen, or if age differences mean that different approaches are needed.

The roles of the professionals at Stage 1

Planning Stage 1

- The plan for Stage 1 contact between the foster carers and adopters should be drafted in consultation with the professional network, the foster carers and the adopters. Foster carers and adopters are likely to have good ideas about what is needed to make the move work well, but they may also feel anxious and this may lead them to over-commit themselves, or to appear inflexible. Social workers who are sensitive to this can promote reflection and self-awareness, and steer a plan that is child-centred but also comfortably achievable for the adults.

- The needs of existing children in both families will have to be taken into account and plans made to include them in the meetings, as and when appropriate. A plan that feels manageable for all concerned and sensitive to the child's needs can be agreed at this stage.[6]

- When the Stage 1 plan has been agreed, it should be made clear that (apart from small adjustments) any proposed changes to it should be referred back to the respective social workers. This enables the responsible social workers to retain their oversight of the process. They will want to discuss the reasons for any proposed changes and follow through those that feel helpful for the child. But they may also need to resist suggestions from foster carers or adopters that the plan should be radically changed, ensuring at all times that the child's needs remain central.

Supporting Stage 1

- The team around the child will need to support and monitor the meetings that are taking place at Stage 1, but it is important to be proportionate in this. Unless difficult issues are emerging, it is probably not necessary for social workers to contact foster carers and adopters after every meeting or contact. Instead, a lighter touch plan of phone availability and/or e-contact might be preferred.

- In some cases, the relationship between the foster carers and the adopters can develop very rapidly, and frequent contact by phone or messaging can be an enjoyable part of Stage 1 for both parties. However, these rapidly developing relationships between the adults can sometimes lead them to make their own adjustments to the plan, overlooking the need to consult with social workers. In such situations, it is possible that, unintentionally, the child's needs become lost in the

---

6   In Scotland, the Children's Hearing should be explicitly informed that there will be flexibility in timescales, led by the emerging needs and responses of the child during the moving period. Following the Hearing, the change in the Compulsory Supervision Order (CSO) would allow all concerned to proceed confidently with the moving plan.

adults' enthusiasm. Social workers need to be alert to this possibility and may need to guide people back to the agreed plan for the child.

- In a small number of cases, foster carers or adopters may express concerns during Stage 1. Foster carers may feel uncertain about the adopters' commitment or capacity to parent the child. Adopters may have concerns about their capacity to care for the child or the capacity of the foster carers to support the child's move. Lower level concerns may be discussed and successfully mediated by the relevant social worker. However, more serious concerns may be indicators of underlying issues that need to be discussed by all of the professionals in the team around the child, and a plan made to address them.

- Key to the success of each of the meetings during Stage 1 is that foster carers and adopters are helped to feel comfortable with the idea of getting to know each other and to understand the value of doing so. It is also important that the professionals communicate well with the families and each other, seeking and sharing feedback and making necessary adjustments. This strengthens the team around the child in readiness for the next critical stage – that of making the move into the adoptive family.

When there are clear indications that the child is feeling familiar and comfortable with the adopters and when the foster carers and the adopters feel confident to proceed, Stage 1 contacts and visits can be drawn to a close and it is time to proceed to the next stage of the UEA Moving to Adoption model: Stage 2: Making the move.

Chapter 5
Stage 2: Making the move

INTRODUCTION

Stage 2 of the UEA Moving to Adoption model covers the period of more intensive visits and contacts that leads up to the child's official move to the adoptive family. Stage 2 begins after the Stage 1 contacts have occurred. Two indicators will determine when it is time to begin Stage 2:

- Firstly, the foster carers and the adopters will have established some trust and rapport and will feel ready to work positively together on the moving plan.

- Secondly, the child will feel comfortable in the presence of the adopters, enjoying their company through playful activities, with the foster carer remaining near at hand.

The dual aims of Stage 2 are firstly for the adopters to feel confident in caring for the child on a daily basis; and secondly, for the child to indicate some trust in the adopters' capacity to meet their needs. These goals are achieved through a series of almost daily contacts between the adopters and the child, enabling the child to experience the adopters as their caregivers across the full range of caregiving tasks. When appropriate levels of confidence and trust have been established, the child is ready to move to the adopters' home. This move marks the end of Stage 2.

Overall, it is important to remember that this period is an intensive one and requires considerable physical and emotional time and energy. The UEA Moving to Adoption pilot study indicated that the maximum manageable period with almost daily visits is about 15 days.

Key principles at Stage 2

- All arrangements and timescales should focus on the needs of the child.

- The child's feelings about the move should be held in mind, and responded to sensitively.

- There should be flexibility in the planning, in consultation with the child, the families and the social workers, to allow for emerging circumstances and needs.

STAGE 2: MAKING THE MOVE

What happens in Stage 2?

The adopters take on caregiving tasks in the foster home

- The moving plan should be structured to allow a series of adopters' visits to the foster home. These should cover each part of the daily routine, including the child waking and going to sleep. There should be planned opportunities for the adopters to share and then take the lead in:

  - making drinks, making and serving food or feeding the child;

  - nappy changing, toileting, bathing, washing and dressing, daytime naps and bedtime routines;

  - offering support when the child needs help;

  - simple outdoor activities that the child is known to enjoy – for example, a short visit to a local park. (NB Long days out, spent in unfamiliar surroundings, are not recommended as they are likely to be physically and emotionally exhausting and to raise the adopters' and the child's anxiety.)

- These practical tasks can best be supported by a foster carer who is able to "coach" the adopters in how to read and respond to the child's verbal and non-verbal signals, for example, how the child's behaviour or appearance might alter when they are tired, or hungry, or worried, and which caregiving approaches are most helpful. This will help the adopters to respond confidently to the child which will, in turn, reduce the child's anxiety.

- Throughout the Stage 2 visits to the foster home, it is important that the foster carer remains physically and/or psychologically available to the child. From the child's perspective, it will feel safer to place their trust in the new parents if, at the same time, they can also trust that their loved and familiar caregivers are "there for them" if needed.

- Skilled foster carers will manage their physical availability with subtlety. For example, initially they may remain in the room while the adopters are feeding the child, but engage themselves in another activity. When the child is comfortable with this, the foster carer may go into another room, with the door left open so that they can be occasionally seen and heard by the child. This flexibility, determined by the child's level of comfort, will enable the child to use both the foster carers and the adopters as a secure base and to gradually trust that the new parents can meet their needs.

- Psychological availability should be managed in ways that allow the child to hold the foster carers in mind when they are apart. For short separations, verbal reassurance can achieve this (for example, during a visit to the park, the adopters might talk gently to the child about going back to (foster carer's name) to have lunch. For longer separations (for example, during an all-day or overnight stay at the adoptive home), a favourite toy from the foster home, photos of the foster family, or an exchange of messages or videos, may be used to reassure the child.

- Trusting relationships between the foster carers and adopters, established in Stage 1, will help the foster carers and adopters to work together and be flexible in their caregiving roles, as this foster carer describes:

    By the time it got to the hands on stage, we knew each other well so it was easy going. If he needed that little bit of reassurance I provided it, passing him back when he settled.

> **EXAMPLE**
>
> **Lucy's move to adoption at 12 months old: a foster carer's diary**
>
> **Stage 2, day 1**
>
> The adopters watched while I fed her in her high chair. Then I stepped back and adoptive mum gave Lucy her yoghurt, which she was delighted about. She adores yoghurt and I knew she would happily allow her new mum to feed her this!

The child's feelings are assessed and responded to

- A key focus for foster carers, adopters and professionals in Stage 2, as in Stage 1, is to tune in to the range of both positive and difficult feelings that the child is likely to be experiencing, and to ensure that these are responded to sensitively. It is important, therefore, that the adults around the child are able to reflect on and respond to their emotional state as Stage 2 progresses.

- Trusting relationships already established in Stage 1 will help all parties to work together in the best interests of the child. This can mean having some flexibility in the plan, in line with changing needs and circumstances, while also keeping a focus on the child's needs and feelings.

- In some cases, the plan may be monitored on a daily basis, with inbuilt flexibility according to the child's emotional progress, as described by this adopter:

    Our baby's feelings were put central. Each day, every adult concerned evaluated how well she was doing – whether we needed to slow things down or speed it up. Brilliantly flexible, but very careful too.

    ### Suggestions for assessing and responding to children's feelings

    - Ensure that the foster carers, adopters and professionals are observing and thinking about the child's emotional state and are taking note of how the child is expressing or not expressing their feelings. Hold in mind that children do not always show their feelings directly.

    - Help children to recognise, name and express positive and difficult feelings both about leaving the foster family and joining the adoptive family. Reflective questions such as, 'I wonder if it feels sad when...', 'I wonder if you're thinking about...' can help children to put their feelings into words.

    - Ensure that there are opportunities to communicate the full range of the child's feelings within the professional network.

    - Help adopters and foster carers to expect and manage signs of anxiety and uncertainty in the child. Encourage them to work together. Initially, the foster carer might need to step forward to comfort the child. Further on in the plan, the foster carer might remain available but support the adopters to provide comfort.

    - Be prepared to slow the pace of the visits if there are signs of distress. The child may need time to have their feelings acknowledged and understood by their trusted adults, before being able to progress towards the move.

    - Ensure that adopters and foster carers have a reflective space in which their thinking and feeling can be shared with professionals and sensitively responded to.

> **EXAMPLE**
>
> **Lucy's move to adoption at 12 months old: a foster carer's diary**
>
> **Stage 2, day 3**
>
> We spent the morning at a local working farm, somewhere Lucy is familiar with. Lucy was upset by the sheep bleating although she usually enjoys this. She appeared very watchful, wary and hyper vigilant, showing signs of regression to how she had been when first placed. It is so hard when a little one is looking to you for reassurance, not to immediately give them the comfort they need. But at this stage it was very important for Lucy to know I was there but to be comforted by her new parents, and she was fine with this.

The child becomes familiar with the adoptive home

- The child's first visit to the adoptive home should be planned on an individual basis. Some older children might need the reassurance of seeing their new home before they start to build trust in the adopters, and a short visit, accompanied by the foster carer, might be made at an early point in Stage 1. Other children might be reassured by seeing photos or a video of the adopters' home, their new bedroom, and so on.

- At the point where the caregiving begins to take place in the adopters' home (for example, when the child first visits for a meal), the role of the foster carer will change. The child needs to experience the (now familiar) adopters as caregivers and to feel their comfort and reassurance at sensitive points such as going to sleep or waking up. The role of the foster carer, therefore, is to encourage the child to feel that the adopters are safe and loving people and that their home is a safe and enjoyable place to be.

- When the child is being placed at a distance, the foster carer's physical presence will need to be supported by the provision of accommodation, either for the foster carers near to the adopters' home or vice versa. Although Stage 2 would typically begin in the foster home, then move to the adopters' home, there may need to be flexibility about this. Consider a wider range of options whilst holding in mind that foster carers need to be emotionally and (as far as possible) physically available to the child.

- Where using booked accommodation, it is preferable to book it for longer than planned so that Stage 2 can be easily extended if necessary.

- There should be a plan for the foster carer's physical presence to reduce gradually, but their psychological presence to remain. Psychological presence can be achieved in a range of ways, for example, photos of the foster carers can be placed prominently in the adoptive home and referred to regularly by the adopters, and the adopters can talk warmly to the child about the foster carers when they are not present. For older children, an early overnight stay with the adopters can be supported by a video call or exchange of messages with the foster carers.

- Each of these steps can help the child to hold the foster carers (and familiar family members, pets, etc) in mind, to know that the foster carers are still thinking and caring about them and to be reassured that they will see the foster carers again soon. The goal is for the child to continue to benefit from the secure base relationship with the foster carers whilst they begin to build secure base relationships with their new parents.

EXAMPLE

Stage 2 visits for Toby (nine months), placed locally (See previous chapter for Stage 1 visits for Toby)

Day 1 Adopter visits 12pm–2pm. Adopter prepares simple lunch, with Toby watching in high chair and foster carer nearby. Offer Toby finger food. Feed dessert if Toby comfortable. Hand over to foster carer if not. Adopter beside foster carer for nappy change and putting Toby in cot for nap.

Day 2 Adopter visits 3pm–5pm. Prepares and serves tea as yesterday. Play on floor with Toby after tea.

Day 3 Adopter visits 10am–12pm. Alongside foster carer when he wakes from morning nap. Adopter changes nappy and dresses Toby for outing. Short outing to swings (very familiar for Toby). Adopter pushes buggy with foster carer beside.

Day 4 Adopter visits 2pm–6pm. Picks Toby up when he wakes from nap. Changes nappy. Brings him downstairs. Foster carer greets him and is in and out of the room. Adopter gives drink and snack. Adopter takes Toby to swings without foster carer. Play in sitting room (foster carer in and out of room). Adopter prepares and serves tea to Toby.

Day 5 Rest day

Day 6 Adopter visits 11am–5pm. Carries out all caregiving tasks during this time, with foster carer available but in the background. Foster carer may give advice on calming Toby if needed or may step forward if Toby is upset and cannot be calmed by the adopter.

Day 7   Adopter arrives 6.15am and attends to Toby as he wakes. Adopter does all caregiving until afternoon nap (to include a visit to the swings without foster carer). Adopter takes a break in the afternoon and returns to prepare and serve Toby's tea. Adopter baths Toby (foster carer in and out of bathroom). Dries and dresses, looks through familiar book. Gives bottle and puts Toby in his cot. Uses same routine as foster carer if he doesn't settle (sit beside cot, hand on his tummy, soft, reassuring words). Foster carer makes judgement about whether or not to intervene if Toby becomes distressed and cannot be settled.

Day 8   Foster carer to bring Toby to adopter's home for 10.30am. Stay, reassure him. Have lunch together. Foster carer to take Toby home after around three hours.

Day 9   Foster carer to take Toby to adopter at 12pm. Leaves when he is settled. Return for review of moving plan meeting at 2.30pm. Foster carer then takes Toby home.

Day 10   Adopter to collect Toby 10–10.30am. Spend the rest of the day at her home, return to foster home for tea and bedtime routine.

Day 11   Adopter collects Toby around 10am and brings him home for the day and overnight. Foster carer to arrive and be there for tea time and bedtime. Foster carer to be available but adopter to do all caregiving tasks.

Day 12   Placement day. Foster carer to phone adopter and go through any issues that have arisen and answer any queries.

EXAMPLE
Stage 2 visits for Fleur (three years), placed at a distance

Week 1   Whole adoptive family (including grandmother) moves in to rented house close to foster home for one week. During this time, the adoptive mother, sometimes accompanied by different family members, spends some time each day with Fleur in the foster family home, or on short local outings. The two families will work out the detail of the plan for each day on a daily basis. By the end of the week, the adoptive mother will have observed and then taken over each part of Fleur's daily routine.

> **End of Week 1** Fleur travels with adoptive family to their home. Whole foster family follow in their car and go to rented accommodation near to the adoptive family for four nights. On the first day, foster mother helps adoptive mother to settle Fleur in her new home. Foster mother stays until Fleur is asleep in the evening. Over subsequent three days, all foster family members have an opportunity to visit the adoptive home once. Foster mother visits each day, gradually reducing her visits to just an hour or two on the last day. The two families will work out the detail of the plan for each day on a daily basis.

The two contrasting case examples above illustrate how the UEA model can be adapted for each child. The particular circumstances of each case have been taken into account to create moving plans that adhere to the key principles of the model.

Applying the key principles during Stage 2, in situations where face-to-face contact can only be minimal

Whilst some level of physical overlap between the two families is optimal for the child, there may be exceptional circumstances where, despite all efforts, only very minimal physical overlap between foster carers and adopters can occur. For example, this may happen when foster carers are unwell or a placement needs to end suddenly because of an emergency.

The risks of children moving where no physical overlap is possible need to be carefully considered alongside the risks to the child of not moving, and decision-making should be clearly recorded.

- If a decision is taken to proceed with the move, special care will need to be taken to maximise the potential of virtual contacts to prepare the child for the move. The range of suggestions for virtual contacts, suggested for Stage 1 (see previous chapter), may be used and adapted to build the child's familiarity and trust in the adopters and to promote some continuity of care. But other elements from Stage 1 that facilitate Stage 2, for example, photos and videos of the adopters, their house and garden, will need to be revisited and can be used for ongoing conversations and reassurance in the final days before the move.

- The key goal of the virtual contact in these situations is to ensure that the child is helped to understand that the adopters will be able to meet their needs for food, comfort and nurture.

- It is also especially important that key information about the child's attachment behaviours, familiar caregiving responses, daily routines, likes and dislikes is passed from the foster carer to the adopters. The social worker may need to take responsibility for ensuring that this information is fully recorded and transferred.

The roles of the professionals at Stage 2

Planning Stage 2

- The Stage 2 contacts between the adopters and the child in the foster home and then in the adoptive home should be drafted in consultation with the professional network and the foster carers and adopters.

- Foster carers and adopters should be empowered to work together to support the child. Their shared commitment to a positive move should be respected and their views and suggestions taken into account. At the same time, the perspectives and wishes of the foster carers and adopters should be heard separately, by their respective social workers. This ensures that the plan is mutually acceptable.

- Stage 2 planning must be sensitive to the needs and circumstances of the adopters and foster carers. Geography, personal characteristics, additional responsibilities and the needs of other family members are all important considerations. Adoption and fostering social workers can ensure that important issues are taken into account for their respective families, but they may also need to promote co-operation and help the two families to understand each other's needs and perspectives.

- Allowing time, within the plan, for rest and reflection can be important for the adults to process the (inevitably) emotionally charged events of Stage 2.

- The plan should be individualised to take into account the specific needs of the child, bearing in mind the Secure Base dimensions. The child's age is one factor, but each child will be different. For example, some babies will take longer than others to comfortably accept caregiving routines from their prospective adopters because they find it hard to trust. An older child who has been with a foster family for some time may need several months to process their losses and adjust to the realities of the new family life – or may be ready to move more quickly.

- The possibility of the plan being adjusted to meet changing needs and circumstances should be held open throughout Stage 2. Unexpected events (illness, extreme weather, family emergencies, etc.) can arise in any situation. Foster carers and adopters should feel empowered to make some adjustments between themselves (for example, to cancel a trip to the park if the weather is unsuitable). But it should also be clear that suggestions for significant changes to the plan (for example, significant changes to the timing of a visit or whether or not the foster carer is to be present during a visit) should be referred to the coordinating social worker (usually in the adoption service). The local authority holds parental responsibility for the child at this stage and it is vital that the appropriate social workers can take ownership of the moving plan and feel confident that the child's needs remain central.

- An interim planning review is an essential element of the planning process in Stage 2. This should draw together the perspectives of all members of the team around the child (and the child themselves, as appropriate). There should be a clear focus on the child's emotional well-being; again, reflecting on the Secure Base dimensions, such as capacity to trust and manage their feelings, will be helpful in planning.

- The decision about the child's readiness to make the move to the adopters will normally be agreed at this point and will depend on the presence of key indicators of the child's developing trust in the adopters. For example, the child should be comfortable to receive food, personal care and nurture from the adopters. They should be able to seek and receive help from the adopters (as appropriate for age and personal characteristics) and appear reasonably relaxed and confident in their new home. Within the moving plan, there should be a shared understanding that the placement day might be deferred to ensure that these indicators are sufficiently established.

Supporting Stage 2

- Social worker contact with the foster carers, adopters and child will need to be more frequent during Stage 2. There will be examples of the child's growing trust in the adopters to share and celebrate, but there may also be strong and sometimes difficult feelings for each party, and these need to be acknowledged and processed with the support of the respective social workers.

- Some foster carers may be anxious that they will not be able to manage their emotions on or around the planned moving day. They may need reassurance that showing emotion is understandable and reflects the care and love that they have offered the child. The social worker can help the foster carer to find the words to explain to the child that their tears mean that they have mixed feelings of sadness (because they will miss the child) and happiness (because they know the child will be loved in their new family).

- In a small number of cases, the foster carers, adopters or child may be having concerns about the move. Good teamwork in the professional network is essential to ensure that any concerns are responded to appropriately and sensitively.

- Fostering and adoption social workers should ensure that they can have private conversations with the foster carers and adopters at key points during Stage 2. Difficult issues can be hard to discuss in the presence of others.

- Adoption social workers should ensure that, in a two-parent couple, both partners are spoken to individually. For a single applicant, it might also be important to speak individually with a key supporter.

- Foster carers and adopters should feel able to contact a social worker at any time. They should be made aware of their own social worker's availability and who should be contacted if they are not available.

The placement day represents a significant milestone, the point at which the child can trust that the adopters can meet their needs, and that they will be safe and nurtured in their new family. However, previous trusting relationships are still important in the child's mind and Stage 3 of the UEA Moving to Adoption model focuses on supporting these relationships after the move.

Chapter 6
Stage 3: Supporting relationships after the move

INTRODUCTION

Stage 3 of the UEA Moving to Adoption model covers the period from the placement day through to the statutory review. The full range of relationships are significant throughout this stage – including those between the adopters and the child, the foster carers and the child, the foster carers and the adopters, and those of the social workers between themselves and with the child and the families. In some cases, the child's and the adopters' relationships with birth family members also need to be supported.

The aim of Stage 3 is to enable the adopters and the child to continue the process of building their relationship, with the child experiencing the adopters as their primary caregivers, while at the same time coming to terms with the loss of the foster carers as their primary caregivers. For foster carers, this stage involves visiting the child within the first few days of their being placed and then their ongoing but gradually decreasing involvement as the child continues to build trust in the new family. This will involve taking on a new role as a supporter of the adoptive family.

> **Key principles at Stage 3**
>
> - Some continuity of foster family relationships and environment will support the child in managing the loss of the foster family and building trust in the adoptive family.
>
> - The child's feelings about the move should be held in mind, and responded to sensitively.
>
> - There should be flexibility in the planning, in consultation with the child, the families and the social workers, to allow for emerging circumstances and needs.

STAGE 3: SUPPORTING RELATIONSHIPS AFTER THE MOVE

What happens in Stage 3?

Placement day

- The placement day (sometimes referred to as moving day) marks the formal beginning of the placement for adoption.

- The UEA model suggests that the placement day is not seen as the ending of the child's relationship with the foster carer. Rather, it is part of the gradual process of the child building trust in the adopters, a process that will continue to be supported by a series of visits from the foster carer, beginning within a few days of the placement day.

- When trusting relationships between the foster carers and the adopters have been built through Stages 1 and 2, the plan for foster carer visits can reduce anxiety for all. The child will be reassured that they will see the foster carer again after the move, foster carers will be reassured to know that they can help the child to settle in their new home, and adopters will be reassured by knowing that they can rely on the foster carer's support and advice during the early days of the placement. In this context, the child's feelings can be acknowledged more openly. For example, this adopter shows empathy for the enormity of his three-year-old's losses as he reflects:

  > *His transition to us would have been very harsh for him without them* [the foster carers] *involved when he made the move. It was essential.*

Providing continuity and enjoying change

After the placement day, there will be many changes for the child to negotiate in every aspect of their life. There are three strands of support for the child that foster carers, adopters and professionals can offer at this stage:

- Firstly, it is important to think sensitively about what the child might be experiencing and feeling and to be alert to the fact that even small differences (for example, a different brand of breakfast cereal) can feel significant and unsettling. Talking about things being different and naming some of the feelings that the child might be experiencing as a result of this can be helpful. Perhaps offering a choice of a familiar and a new cereal may help the child to understand that some things can stay the same and other things can change. Both are OK and the child can exercise some choice in the pace of any change.

- Secondly, providing continuity of environment, where possible, can reduce the child's anxiety. With this in mind, it is common practice for adopters, in consultation with the foster carers, to provide some continuity of the sensory environment after the move – continuity of bedding (unwashed) and clothing from the foster home, the use of the same laundry powder, bedtime routines, toys, rhymes, stories and songs are all positive examples of this. Over time, the child can then be given opportunities to experience new options, again at their own pace.

- Thirdly, it is important for children to be helped to experience additional pleasures and enjoyable experiences in their new family. For example, in the UEA Moving to Adoption pilot project, a six-year-old enjoyed Lego and was excited by a new Lego set waiting for him in his adoptive home, along with a special nightlight, and a special shelf for his toys. A three-year-old valued his foster carers' commitment to send him updated photos of their pets after the move – and was also thrilled by his new toys.

In summary, good practice at this stage involves a sensitive attunement to the changes that have occurred for the child, some continuity of environment where possible, *and* a spirit of enjoying and looking forward, as the following adopter describes:

> *His bedroom was much bigger than his old one so we filled it with his belongings and photos. We put similar wall stickers up and photos of his foster carers and siblings next to his bed. We talked about things being different and how he might be feeling. We had a lot of fun with his new toys. He settled into his bedroom well.*

Foster carer has contact with the child immediately post-placement

- The moving plan should be structured to allow a series of foster carer visits and contacts with the child and the adopters in the days and weeks after the placement day. The purpose of this contact is to support the child's growing trust in the adopters. There are various ways in which foster carer visits and contacts can achieve this:

  - The child's anxiety is reduced by the foster carer visiting the adoptive home. The adopters can provide verbal reassurance that this will happen and older children can benefit by having a chart or calendar that shows when the next visit is due.

  - The child is reassured by seeing that loved adults do not simply "disappear" and that they continue to show their care and interest. In the child's mind, this may reduce the risk that the adopters might "disappear" in a similar way.

  - The adopters' anxiety is reduced by knowing that the foster carer is available to provide advice on caregiving, if requested. When the adopters' anxiety is reduced in this way, they are likely to be more available to the child, helping them to settle and enjoy their new surroundings.

- The foster carer can demonstrate pleasure and enjoyment of the new environment of the adopters' home.

- The foster carer can demonstrate trust in the adopters as the caregivers of the child, helping the child also to develop trust in them.

- By the beginning of Stage 3, the adopters will have gained confidence as caregivers for the child. They will be familiar with the child's routines and preferences and will have learned strategies to calm and reassure the child when needed. With this foundation in place, it is important that once the move has been made, the child experiences the adopters as their primary caregivers and that the foster carer visits support the new adoptive relationships.

- The role of the foster carer during the visits, therefore, is that of a warm and encouraging supporter of the adoptive family. Visits should be time-limited and purposeful (e.g. a cup of tea, a chat and a short play) and not involve the foster carer undertaking caregiving tasks.

- Some adopters and foster carers may be uncertain about what should be talked about with the child or when the child is present. For example, foster carers may be unsure about whether to refer to other foster family members or other elements of the child's life in their family, as they may worry that this will upset the child. Talking through these concerns with the social worker in advance can help foster carers and adopters to feel more confident and relaxed during the visits.

- The frequency and nature of the visits should be individualised, primarily according to the needs of the child but also shaped by the capacities of the foster carers to support the adoptive family and the relationship that has developed between the foster carers and adopters.

- A child with a history of anxiety around change may need to be reassured by the physical presence of the foster mother during part of every day for the first few days. For example, this might involve being present for most of the first day, staying locally to facilitate an early visit the next day, and then a sequence of visits, gradually reducing in time and frequency.

- An older child may be more able to hold the foster carer in mind when they are apart and feel reassured by planned video calls interspersed with visits. For instance, one three-year-old child was reassured by the foster carers sending a video each evening, in which they were waving, smiling, saying 'goodnight, sleep tight', 'thinking of you' and 'see you soon'. The adopters were able to show this to the child before their bedtime routine and felt it to be extremely helpful.

- This fostering social worker summarises her thoughts on the benefits of the foster carer visits for both the child and the adopters:

  Contact with foster carers helped adopters meet the child's needs with confidence whilst also accepting guidance on issues they were faced with. This provided the child with continuity and a familiar approach which helped the child be reassured their needs would be met and his trust in adopters to develop.

EXAMPLE

Lucy's move to adoption at 12 months old: a foster carer's diary

It was so wonderful to see the huge beaming smile and excited look on Lucy's face when I walked in the day after moving day. She put up her hands for a cuddle and my heart melted. This quickly changed to her looking around, confused, a little unsettled and for the first 20 minutes she really didn't know whether she wanted to be with me, Daddy or Mummy. A perfectly normal reaction at this stage – it not only showed her attachment to me but also the growing bond and trust with her adoptive family. She was then happy to play on the floor and move between us while we chatted and had coffee.

Applying the key principles during Stage 3, in situations where face-to-face contact is difficult to achieve

In a small number of cases, a mutually agreed plan for face-to-face Stage 3 contacts with the foster carer may be difficult to achieve. In these cases, face-to-face contacts may need to be complemented or even replaced by a robust plan for virtual contacts. But as in Stages 1 and 2, the key principles can be used to underpin creative planning and practice.

This plan should be individualised, according to the needs of the child, and a range of media may be used. For example, this could be through video calls, recording and sending videos, the foster carer sending cards through the post, or the adopters ensuring that photos of the foster family are readily available as prompts for gentle conversations about them.

For video or audio calls, as with face-to-face contact, it is helpful to engage the foster carer and adopters in planning the calls to ensure that they are purposeful and meet specific needs. For example:

- calls between the foster carer and the adopters that aim to help the adopters to build their relationship with the child and achieve continuity of care;

- calls that include the child and aim to help them to know that their foster carer is still holding them in mind and is supportive of the placement;

- calls that include other children in the foster home and have the dual aim of reassuring these children that the child is settling in their new home and reassuring the child that their foster siblings are still holding them in mind and are supportive of the placement.

Helping the child to manage feelings around foster carer visits

- Children will show a range of reactions to the foster carer visits. Some may show pleasure at seeing the foster carer, appear to enjoy the visit and show no particular distress on parting. This may be associated with positive relationships having been established between the foster carer and the adopters during Stages 1 and 2, as this adoptive father of a one-year-old describes:

  He recognised her [the foster mother] *and was happy to see her, but was not clingy and just played with all of us or with his toys. It was like he felt it was normal to have all of us there relaxing like we did during our visits to the foster home.*

- Other children may look to the foster carer for comfort and nurture in the early visits. For example, a baby might reach out to be held by the foster carer, or crawl across the room to her. This can create both positive and more difficult feelings for the foster carer and the adopter. For the child, the most helpful response might be for the foster carer to offer a hug and some warm words, and then gently encourage the child to reconnect with the adopter.

- When a child is confused or distressed by the foster carer visits, this will need to be carefully explored by all of the adults involved. It is important to remember that difficult feelings connected with separation and loss are wholly understandable at this stage and when they are shown overtly, they provide opportunities for the adopters to provide reassure and comfort, as this adoptive mother describes:

  The visits were definitely helpful. They allowed him to express his feelings (i.e. that he missed the foster carers) *and be reassured, allowed him to know he was still thought about and cared about.*

- In all cases, the foster carer visits will need sensitive handling from the foster carers and adopters, supported by their social workers. Adopters and foster carers may need focused social work support to help them to work together to tune in to the child's feelings and respond sensitively to them.

- Positive relationships built in Stages 1 and 2 can promote flexible "tweaking" of the plan to help the child to manage their feelings. For example, a foster carer visit might end in a local park, so that, having acknowledged the sadness of the parting, the adopters and child can move on together to share an enjoyable activity.

> **EXAMPLE**
>
> **Supporting a five-year-old child's relationship with her foster carer after the move**
>
> Mia enjoyed her foster carer's visits, but on one occasion pulled the scarf from her foster carer's neck and was reluctant to part with it. With the adopter's agreement, the foster carer allowed her to keep it. The adopter found the scarf in Mia's bed the next morning and used it to talk about love and loss. The adopter reported that Mia seemed to move on emotionally after this and show greater trust and affection in her adoptive family.

Foster carer has contact with the child in the longer term

- After the first six weeks of the adoptive placement, it is to be hoped and expected that the child's trust in the adopters will be developing and any visits or contacts with the foster carer planned beyond this point will have a different purpose and value for the child.

- Firstly, there is the ongoing comfort for the child of knowing that they were loved and valued in the foster home and that the foster family continues to hold them in mind and shows interest in their lives. Secondly, ongoing visits or contact can be important for the child's future sense of identity, providing information about the child's early months and years, deepening understandings of birth family members and increasing the sense of continuity in the child's life story.

> **EXAMPLE**
>
> **A foster carer describes some benefits of contact with the adoptive family in the longer term**
>
> *At the age of three, Amy moved from my care to her adoptive family after previously being placed with two different foster carers. After the planned visits, we all kept in touch quite regularly. This was of immense benefit to Amy as she had many unanswered questions as she grew older. An example of this was when Amy asked her adoptive mum to contact me to find out if I collected her from her previous foster carer or if the carer had brought her to my house. This information was important to Amy, and it was the beginning of many further questions about her early life. Another piece of the jigsaw puzzle of her life was slotted into place, which would never have been possible if we hadn't kept in touch with her adopters.*

The roles of the professionals at Stage 3

Planning Stage 3

- The plan for the placement day and the Stage 3 contacts between the foster carer and the child in the adoptive home should be drafted in consultation with the professional network and the foster carers and adopters.

- External factors, such as geography or the needs of other children in the foster family, must be taken into account when planning the foster carer visits. When the local authority can offer allowances to the foster carer for a period after the move, in acknowledgement of the additional time and tasks involved, this can provide necessary practical support as well as a welcome recognition of the importance of this stage of the moving process.

- The possibility of the plan being adjusted to meet changing needs and circumstances should be held open throughout Stage 3. As in Stage 2, foster carers and adopters should feel empowered to make small adjustments between themselves, but it should also be clear that suggestions for significant changes to the plan should be referred to the social workers, and the role of the adoption or child's social worker as the co-ordinator of the plan should remain clear.

- In a small number of cases, if the foster carers or adopters report very difficult feelings around the visits for themselves or the child, and these feelings appear unmanageable, even with skilled social work support, it may be necessary to end the visits. Important here is that the child is gently told that the visits have come to an end, preferably by the foster carers and the adopters together, and that the child is reassured that the foster carer will continue to care about them and hold them in mind. Practical examples or evidence can help here; for example, the child knowing that the foster carers have kept a nice photo of them, as they have of other children whom they cared for. A range of indirect contact might be considered to reinforce this message.

SUPPORT FOR ALL PARTIES AT STAGE 3 AND BEYOND

This section considers the range of post-placement support that may be needed by foster carers, adopters and children. Individuals within each of these groups are likely to have changing needs as their roles and relationships are reconfigured by the adoption process, and they may need sensitive and timely professional support, both immediately after the move and in the years ahead.

Support for foster carers

The moving period is usually an intense and tiring time for foster families. There may be strong personal emotions to be managed, and these feelings may endure or deepen after the move. It is important for social workers to take into account the needs and feelings of *all* foster family members, and one-to-one sessions may help individuals to express their particular needs and feelings.

The full range of feelings may be apparent in the foster family. As well as sadness and loss, there may be relief when a problematic placement has ended, happiness that the child will be secure and loved in the new family, or sometimes anxiety that this may not be the case.

Suggestions for supporting foster carers after the move

- Enable foster carers to feel listened to and understood and to know that their grief and sadness, and perhaps that of other children in the household, is legitimate and to be expected in these circumstances.

- Where foster carers feel unable to manage their emotions and become overwhelmed during visits from/to the adopters and child, it may be necessary to adjust the plan to something more manageable for all. For example, a park meeting might be less stressful than a home visit.

- Help foster carers to think about the importance of this move for the child and to take satisfaction from the good job that they have done in loving and supporting the child's healthy developmental progress in placement and the successful move to a new family.

- Pairing foster carers with an experienced peer (a "buddy" system) can provide this form of support, but it is also important that foster carers feel supported and listened to by their social worker and agency.

- Provide training and support that acknowledges and prepares foster carers for the mixed feelings, including grief, that they may experience. Adopters and other professionals can also benefit from these understandings.

- Ensure that fostering social workers understand their role in understanding and legitimising the full range of foster carers' feelings after the move, and that this may be key in helping the foster family to recover from the loss of the child. In all cases, before further placements are considered, it is important for the social worker to feel confident that all family members are physically and emotionally ready to provide secure base caregiving for a new child in the family.

Support for adopters

The early weeks of an adoption placement can also involve a complex mix of positive and difficult feelings and responses for adopters. As well as happiness and excitement, anxiety, loss of identity, loneliness, disappointment, low mood and physical symptoms are common.

Suggestions for supporting adopters after the move

- Hold in mind the possibility of depressive symptoms in the adopters, in the light of unfulfilled expectations of self, the child, friends and family or professionals, and present them as understandable and to be expected in the context of the major life changes created by adoption.

- Use gentle statements and questions to normalise the situation and open conversations with adopters. For example, 'It's normal to take time to bond with a child. What activities are you enjoying with them at the moment? What's not going so well?'

- In addition to the planned social worker visits, adopters should be made aware of their own social worker's availability and who should be contacted if they are not available.

- Underline the need for self-care approaches, and to seek medical support if necessary.

- Ensure that pre-adoption training and support address the feelings that adopters may experience and ways these may be managed.

Supporting the adopters to provide a secure base for the child

- The key task for adopters in Stage 3 is to provide secure base caregiving that will help the child to develop their trust and sense of security and belonging in the adoptive family.

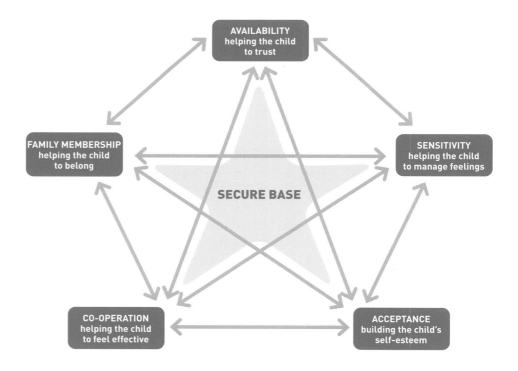

- In the early weeks of the placement, adopters can be supported to think about parenting approaches that reflect each of these parenting dimensions and how they might be individualised in ways that are acceptable for their particular child. For example, for a child who does not seem comfortable with the physical closeness of sitting on a lap, availability might be demonstrated by sitting beside the child on the sofa to share a book or a toy.

- Building the child's adoptive family identity and helping them to enjoy their new experiences and relationships will be an important focus during the early weeks. Adopters can also be supported to think sensitively about how the child might be thinking and feeling about the separation from the foster family, and how to help the child to acknowledge, name and manage these feelings.

- As the placement progresses, adopters can be supported to reflect on their child's previous relationships and identities in their birth family, and to think about the impact of these on the child. For example, they may be supported to:

  - think about the ways in which previous caregivers have breached or built the child's trust and how this may have shaped the child's expectations of adults;

  - show sensitivity to the child's thinking and feeling about their birth family relationships and identity, and help the child to acknowledge, name and manage these feelings;

  - show non-judgemental acceptance of both the strengths and difficulties of the birth family, helping the child to build a positive sense of their birth family identity.

- It is important for adopters to demonstrate co-operation by working together with the child to set firm boundaries, but having some flexibility within them, allowing the child some safe and appropriate choice and agency, and understanding that the child's needs and understandings will change through different developmental stages.

- Finally, in relation to family membership, as well as building a positive adoptive family identity, adopters need to help the child to establish a comfortable sense of their birth family identity, mediated on an individualised basis, through the full range of contact arrangements from no contact through to regular face-to-face meetings. Again, children's needs and feelings about their birth family identity and relationships, including with siblings they have been separated from, are likely to change over time and adopters will need to be alert and responsive to this.

Support for children

Children moving from a foster family to a new adoptive family will experience a range of feelings immediately after the placement, or later on as the new arrangements settle into place. For some children, there will be an early sense of security and trust that progresses evenly and positively. For others, growing affection for adopters may be accompanied by feelings of guilt and confusion. Most are likely to experience a sense of loss of previous foster family or birth family relationships and to have some feelings of sadness and grief.

For some children, their behaviour and capacity to manage their emotions may regress, with problems re-emerging around eating, sleeping and toileting that can be upsetting to the child as well as to the adopters. The child will need reassuring that this is quite normal after a big change and given confidence that these problems will resolve as they settle in.

Whether immediately post-placement, or later on in the adoption, the child's relationship with the social worker can have a unique value for the child and can make a distinct contribution to the child's secure base. The social worker in this context is in the position of being able to hold all of the aspects of a child's life together. They have knowledge (either directly or through files) both of the child's external world (for example, their previous history and relationships) and, through direct work, their inner world (for example, their memories, beliefs and feelings about the past). If the social worker can help to bring together and make sense of the external and internal worlds of the child in this way and in themselves offer predictability and continuity, the relationship with the child will be key in helping the child to feel more secure and more competent (Schofield, 2005).

Suggestions for supporting children post-placement

- Remember that children appear to dip in and out of feelings of sadness and grief. They can be intensely sad at one moment, then suddenly switch to playing happily the next. This may lead adults to believe children are unaffected, or that the sadness isn't genuine, but it is important to bear in mind that "puddle jumping" powerful feelings in this way is a defence mechanism that prevents children from being overwhelmed by them.

- Hold in mind that children do not always show their feelings directly, for example, children who are angry or worried may become controlling/ rejecting towards close adults. Sadness and loss may be expressed through difficult behaviour or regression in their development. Some avoid their painful feelings and appear "fine", but at the same time, are rather remote and disconnected from their new parents.

- Listen to the child. This includes ascertaining their wishes and feelings, but also ascertaining the meanings that the child has attached to people and experiences. The social worker can, though, try to see the world through the child's eyes in order both to understand what the child is thinking and to help them make sense of the external world. The social worker can share both the sadness and loss that the child may be feeling, and also the pleasures and good things in the new family.

- Be aware of the balance between being directive regarding the child's needs and relinquishing all parental autonomy to the adopters. Adopters need to feel a sense of being respected and valued as the child's parents as well as feeling held and supported by a knowledgeable professional. Social work supervisors can help social workers to reflect on and clarify their role across this dimension.

> **EXAMPLE**
>
> This foster carer describes the way in which a child's important relationship with her birth mother was understood and acknowledged in the foster family and then in her adoptive family.
>
> *Abbie had a photo that was taken at the contact centre, of herself with her mummy. Her mummy had actually taken the photo and had it framed and gave it to her. And it stayed in her bedroom for quite a long time. Then one day she brought it downstairs and put it with our family photos. And interestingly enough, when she moved* [to her adoptive family] *she did exactly the same. She had her photo of herself and her mummy on her bedroom windowsill at her adopter's house, and the adopter said that about nine months after she'd moved she brought that photo downstairs and put it with the family photos.*
>
> This example demonstrates the value of several Secure Base dimensions. *Sensitivity* and *acceptance* have enabled the child to express their feelings, feel effective and make decisions, while also finding that her need for *belonging* to more than one family is acknowledged and valued in both her foster and adoptive families.

The UEA Moving to Adoption model provides a framework for supporting children's moves to adoption and also addressing the needs of foster carers and adopters before, during and after the move. For some agencies this will involve small adjustments to existing practice; for others, more significant changes will be needed. The following chapter focuses on the implementation of the UEA model in practice, and provides links to online resources that can support implementation.

Chapter 7
Implementing the UEA Moving to Adoption model

INTRODUCTION

The implementation of a new practice approach in child and family social work invariably brings both challenges and rewards for the individual practitioner and their team, and also the inter-professional network and the wider organisation.

In the field of adoption practice, there is a great deal of emotional as well as professional investment. Adoption addresses the long-term future for vulnerable children. Carefully selected adopters will make a lifelong commitment as the parents of a child, and the child's birth family and foster family relationships will change irrevocably. Adoption, therefore, is a high stakes activity, and it is both likely and understandable that proposed changes in practice will require new knowledge and skills but also cause some anxiety for those concerned. The UEA Moving to Adoption model infers changes in thinking and practice across the whole organisation and if the implementation of the model is to be successful, it is important that these anxieties are addressed and that the changes are carefully thought through and managed.

There are various components in the successful implementation of change in an organisation, and this chapter considers these components in relation to the implementation of the UEA Moving to Adoption model. Firstly, it is suggested that a plan to introduce and discuss the new approach at each level of the organisation can help all involved to feel invested in the proposed changes. A professional culture that is not critical of former practice, but instead encourages some flexibility and creativity of approach, can help people at every level to feel more involved, empowered and committed to taking things forward. When the changes have been absorbed into practice, they will need to be reviewed and adjusted over time to ensure that they are working well for all concerned. Finally, an ongoing programme of training, discussion and review of the changes will help to embed and sustain the new practice and to ensure that it is responding to other changes and developments in the organisation.

Agencies that are planning to implement the UEA model may need to respond to a range of questions from the different stakeholders involved in supporting children's moves to adoption. To help with this, some frequently asked questions are listed later in the chapter, and some suggested responses provided.

The chapter closes by introducing the concept of the team as a secure base. This recognises that professionals involved in complex and demanding work such as moving a child to adoption need to be able to rely on their supervisors and colleagues for structured and informal support and guidance. The Secure Base model provides a framework for thinking about this and here it is applied in the context of planning and supporting a child's move to adoption.

FAMILIARISING THE ADOPTION SERVICE WITH THE MODEL

A first step in implementing the UEA Moving to Adoption model is to ensure that all staff within the adoption service, including the adoption panel members, are familiar with the model and also have an understanding of the research and theory that inform it. Opportunities for discussion and reflection are important, as people think through the implications of applying the model and the changes in practice that it may bring. There will be agency and regional variation in the ways in which the model is applied, but the aim is for all staff and panel members to feel confident that the principles of the model are sound and to be committed to working flexibly within them.

The UEA Moving to Adoption model is underpinned by the Secure Base model. It is important for adopters, staff and panel members to have an understanding of this framework for therapeutic caregiving and for the language, principles and practice of the Secure Base model to be established as an integral part of the adoption service. Information, training modules and practice resources associated with the Secure Base model can be found at https://www.uea.ac.uk/groups-and-centres/centre-for-research-on-children-and-families/secure-base-model.

Suggestions for familiarising the adoption service with the model

- The *UEA Moving to Adoption Key Principles* leaflet is a good starting point for all adoption service staff and panel members to begin their understanding of the model. This leaflet can be downloaded from https://www.movingtoadoption.co.uk/and is suitable for office printing.

- *An Introduction to the UEA Moving to Adoption Model* is a PowerPoint presentation, including trainer notes, that can be used flexibly to introduce adoption staff and panel members to the model. It is downloadable from the Moving to Adoption website. The session covers some background theory and research, and provides an explanation of the model, including benefits and challenges. It also invites participants to think about specific implementation issues for their service and how best to manage them. In addition, the 'Resources' section of the website contains a link to a 20-minute video setting out the research and theory that underpins the model (https://www.movingtoadoption.co.uk/wp-content/uploads/2020/11/Beth-Neil-Sept-2020.mp4).

  This training session may be used flexibly within teams or across the whole adoption service to ensure that all staff are familiar with the model and have had a chance to discuss its potential impact on their particular role. It may also be used for ongoing training/induction of new members of staff and/or adoption panel members.

- Regional adoption agencies (RAAs) will need to work closely with their voluntary agency partners, preferably with key representatives from these agencies as part of their working group.

- A small group of managers and practitioners who have a special interest in this area of work might be appointed as a working group tasked with leading discussions, disseminating information and responding to queries as implementation proceeds.

FAMILIARISING KEY PROFESSIONALS WITH THE MODEL

Key professionals in this context include fostering social workers and managers, children's social workers and managers, independent reviewing officers (IROs) and therapists. In Scotland, because of the involvement of the Children's Hearing system in agreeing the child's move, it will also be helpful for professionals working within this system to be familiar with the model.

Successful implementation relies on each of these groups being informed about the model and the rationale for using it from an early stage. They will also need opportunities to think through and discuss the implications for their particular area of practice.

It is important that all key professionals are allready familiar with the language, principles and practice of the Secure Base model as this will further their understanding of the Moving to Adoption model. In the case of fostering managers, social workers and support workers, familiarity with the Secure Base model is especially important. Where not already the case, it is recommended that the Secure Base model is established as an integral part of the fostering service, with foster carers receiving Secure Base training and the model embedded in foster carer reviews, support and supervision. Information, training modules and practice resources can be found at: https://www.uea.ac.uk/groups-and-centres/centre-for-research-on-children-and-families/secure-base-model.

Independent fostering services that work with the adoption agency will also need information about the UEA Moving to Adoption model, as there may be implications for the commissioning process. For example, an important element of the model is the recognition that the child's relationship with their foster carer will need to be supported after the adoption placement, and the foster carer's post-placement availability may need to be discussed at management level once the adoption plan has been made.

It is helpful to consider a range of approaches to familiarising key professionals with the model. For example:

- a launch event or conference: ideally this would include presentations from social workers, foster carers and adopters who have had experience of working with the model. If this is not possible, case studies can be found in Chapters 4, 5 and 6 of this book;
- a presentation to managers of these professional groups;
- a presentation to key groups or teams;
- circulation of the link to the Moving to Adoption website (https://www.movingtoadoption.co.uk/), highlighting key resources within it.

FAMILIARISING FOSTER CARERS WITH THE MODEL

The capacity of foster carers to work with adopters and professionals within the principles of the model is key to successful implementation. It is important, therefore, that they receive training on the model, and have opportunities to discuss the changes in practice that it may bring, along with the likely impact on themselves and their families.

Foster carers may vary in how much they welcome the changes. The UEA pilot project found that the large majority welcomed the adjustment to their practice, finding that it very much aligned with what they felt to be in the best interests of the children. There is the potential, however, for some foster carers to be resistant to the changes, and perhaps to perceive them as a criticism of their past practice. All foster carers therefore will need reassurance that everyone in the service is learning and developing in this area, that the model recommends working together and discussion with foster carers throughout, and that they will be listened to and supported at each stage.

Preparing a Child for Adoption and Supporting the Move: The role of foster carers is a PowerPoint presentation, including trainer notes, that can be used flexibly to introduce foster carers to the model. It is downloadable from https://www.movingtoadoption.co.uk/. The session firstly outlines the importance of providing a secure base for the child in short-term foster care. It then provides the background theory and research to the model, and an explanation of it, from the foster carer perspective. It also promotes discussion about the emotional and practical issues for foster carers who are working within the principles of the model.

Agencies might choose to develop an information pack on the model to send to foster carers at the point of matching. Fostering social workers and foster carers might use the *UEA Moving to Adoption: Key Principles leaflet* as a helpful basis for discussion in support and supervision sessions. This document can be downloaded from https://www.movingtoadoption.co.uk/ and is suitable for office printing.

FAMILIARISING ADOPTERS WITH THE MODEL

Prospective adopters will need to be prepared for their role in working with foster carers and professionals within the principles of the model. They may be introduced to the model and its underlying principles in their preparatory training. Post-approval/pre-placement workshops might also be offered.

Supporting a Child's Move to Adoption: The role of adopters is a PowerPoint presentation, including trainer notes, that can be used flexibly to introduce prospective adopters to the model. It is downloadable from https://www.movingtoadoption.co.uk/. The session outlines the background theory and research to the model, and provides an explanation of it, from the adopter perspective. It also promotes discussion about the emotional and practical issues for adopters who are supporting a child's move within the principles of the model, and provides pointers to building a secure base in their family after the move has occurred.

Agencies might choose to develop an information pack on the model to send to adopters at the point of matching. Adoption social workers and prospective adopters might find the *UEA Moving to Adoption: Key Principles leaflet* helpful as a basis for discussion during assessment or post approval visits. This document can be downloaded from https://www.movingtoadoption.co.uk/and is suitable for office printing.

SOME FREQUENTLY ASKED QUESTIONS

The following are examples of questions that have commonly been asked by professionals, foster carers and adopters who are developing their understanding of the UEA Moving to Adoption model.

What might be the benefits of the UEA Moving to Adoption model compared to traditional practice?

We know that adoption has provided high levels of security and permanence for children who have been in care (Thomas, 2013; Palacios *et al*, 2019). However, ongoing developmental challenges for children and stresses for adopters are common, and are elevated compared to children in the general population (Selwyn *et al*, 2015; Neil, Young and Hartley, 2018). This is linked to a wide range of factors, including the child's age at placement and adverse experiences prior to being adopted. There is some evidence that one factor linked to less positive outcomes for adopted children is the quality of the child's transition from foster care into the adoptive home (Selwyn *et al*, 2015; Neil *et al*, 2020).

It is clear, therefore, that the transition from foster care to adoption makes a significant contribution to the outcome of the adoption and that traditional transition practice may not have always recognised this. It is important that we apply new knowledge and understanding of positive practice in supporting children's moves to form moving plans that are responsive to the particular needs of each and every child.

Evidence from the two adoption agencies that took part in the UEA pilot study (Neil, Young and Hartley, 2018) suggests that the Moving to Adoption model is responsive to individual children's needs and that this is seen as a key benefit to the child and to the move overall. The UEA team gathered feedback from adoption, fostering and children's social workers, foster carers and adopters, which showed that the majority of people in each group felt that the move had gone well and there was a high level of satisfaction with the model across all groups.

How does the Secure Base model connect with the UEA model of moving a child to adoption?

The Secure Base model is based in attachment theory and research into foster care and adoption, and is already well established as a useful tool for fostering and adoption practice. It can help social workers, foster carers and adopters to identify developmental strengths or needs in the child and also the particular caregiving responses that will be effective during each stage of the move. It also helps to identify caregiving strengths and difficulties in foster carers and adopters that may be relevant for a particular child, and thus supports better informed planning for the move using the UEA model. Furthermore, it provides a well-respected and shared language for reporting on the plan to LAC reviews, the adoption panel and the courts.

Does using the model involve more social work time?

At Stage 1 (Getting to know each other), the team around the child will need to support and monitor the meetings and contacts that are taking place between the families. However, it is important to be proportionate with this work. Unless difficult issues are emerging, it is not usually necessary for social workers to contact foster carers and adopters after every meeting. Instead, a lighter touch plan of telephone availability and/ or e-contact might be preferred.

At Stage 2 (Making the move), a more intensive level of support and monitoring will be needed. There will be almost daily visits or contact between the adopters, foster carers and child during this stage, and the respective social workers will need to check in on each of them to monitor the child's progress in building trust, discuss how each of the parties is feeling, and pick up on any practical issues that are emerging. Managers would need to supervise this work in the usual way.

At Stage 3 (Supporting relationships after the move), the team around the child will need to continue to work together to ensure that the foster carers and adopters are comfortable with the plan, and confident of their roles within it, and that the child's needs are being understood and met. Some flexibility may be required to accommodate changing needs and circumstances. This stage may require some additional social work time as there is likely to be a longer period of contact between the foster carer and the adoptive family than in traditional practice. Managers would need to supervise this work in the usual way.

At all stages, social worker availability is important, along with clear plans (shared with the whole team around the child) for who should be contacted when the social worker is not available.

Social workers and supervisors may need additional time for reflective supervision in the early stages of introducing the model. The model requires individualised planning for each placement and this will need to be discussed and thought through. In addition, moving away from familiar practice to practice that is more flexible can feel unsettling and require additional support.

How have foster carers, adopters and other professionals found using the model?

The UEA pilot project found that the large majority of professionals, foster carers and adopters considered the model to be positive, helpful and straightforward to understand. For most, it chimed with established good practice in other areas of working with children and with their understandings of how best to support children through change in other areas of their lives.

Some professionals, foster carers or adopters might feel uncertain and find it difficult to trust a new model of practice, but with help and discussion of the principles, they may understand how it could be beneficial and be willing to try it.

There may be occasional situations where, despite good preparation and support, a professional, foster carer or adopter finds it difficult to accept certain aspects of the model. In these cases, it remains important to adhere to the principles of the UEA model and to adjust the plan accordingly. For example, if foster carer visits after the move prove impossible, the principle 'Some continuity of foster family relationships and environment will support the child in managing the loss of the foster family and building trust in the adoptive family' may be addressed by a plan for some structured virtual contact that has been discussed and agreed by the foster carers and adopters.

What if I find the plan for a move isn't working, at any stage?

Flexibility is at the heart of the model. If at any stage (after consultation with all parties) it is clear that the plan needs to be changed to meet the child's needs, or provide better support for foster carers or adopters, there should be a review of the plan and adjustments made accordingly. It might be helpful to consider the question, 'What is the best possible way to move things forward, whilst still working within the principles of the model?'

What are the best ways to embed and sustain the model?

Review and adjust agency documentation, policies and procedures to ensure that the language, principles and practice of the Moving to Adoption model are fully embedded in the adoption service. The goal is for the model to be flagged as part of the service at all levels, rather than simply a supplementary piece of practice to be introduced only when children are moved.

Ideas for embedding and sustaining the model include:

- Consider the agency policies and procedures for the matching and placement of children. Issues might include arrangements for the payment of foster carers moving children to adoption, and the process for ending fostering placements and beginning adoptive placements.

- Review documentation, including website information, publicity leaflets, preparation and other training content, matching reports, placement plans and post-adoption support plans.

- Include expectations around supporting children's moves as part of the conversation with adopters throughout the assessment process. Some understanding of the key principles should be reflected in the Prospective Adopter's Report (PAR) completed for the adoption panel.

- Use key meetings during the moving process, for example, Placement Meetings and Reviews of Transitions, as opportunities for the team around the child to reflect on how the key principles are being applied, and how this is working for the individual child, with adjustments made accordingly.

- Use the model as a framework for discussion in individual supervision and group supervision. Possible questions for discussion might be, 'What were the benefits of using the model in this case? What were the challenges and how were they overcome?' There might also be discussions on the extent to which the Secure Base model helped to support the move to adoption.

- Find ways of continuing to grow and develop professional understanding of the model. For example:

  - Suggest that the implementation/working group continues to share information, articles, and ideas from other adoption agencies with colleagues.

  - Make a note of cases where the model has worked well or where there have been some challenges. These cases can be shared with staff for reflection and discussion. Implementation requires a learning process in the organisation and this will be most effective if achieved through discussion of cases and practice.

  - Review the use of the model each year (or more frequently at first) in team meetings, seminars, and so on.

  - Repeat training/provide induction in the model for new panel members, foster carers, adopters and professionals.

  - Include an exploration of the Moving to Adoption website (www.movingtoadoption.co.uk) as part of the induction programme for new staff and panel members.

  - Seek feedback on the model from professionals, foster carers and adopters, and use this to support or adjust practice.

THE ORGANISATION AS A SECURE BASE FOR PROFESSIONALS

Moving a child to adoption involves the making and breaking of caregiving relationships and has lifelong repercussions for all involved. The professionals involved with the move will have invested, variously, in the well-being of the child, the birth parents, the foster carers and the adopters. They may also have a personal connection to the issues of identity, separation, loss and grief, which the move will entail. It is worth remembering here Bowlby's meaning of a secure base as 'a secure base for exploration'; a successful adoption agency, therefore, should have strategies to enable professionals to feel safe to explore their ideas, feelings and practice at each stage of the planning and the move.

Firstly, social workers and other professionals need to be able to rely on a secure base relationship with a trusted supervisor or manager. In addition, secure base relationships with peers can act as a foundation for effective team working, which becomes especially important during the intensive period of work around a child's move to adoption.

The five dimensions of the Secure Base model can be used as a framework for thinking about these varied strands of support for social workers, from managers, supervisors and peers (Biggart *et al*, 2017). For further information, see the 'Secure Base in Teams' section of the Secure Base website: https://www.uea.ac.uk/groups-and-centres/centre-for-research-on-children-and-families/secure-base-model.

- **Availability – builds trust**
  At each stage of the child's move, anxiety can be a dominant feeling for professionals, and this can affect their capacity to be physically and emotionally available for foster carers, adopters and children. When the social worker can trust in the availability of a reliable and supportive supervisor, their anxiety is reduced and they feel safe and protected in their work. This, in turn, frees the social worker to "be there" physically and emotionally for the person they are supporting. Feeling safe and supported in their work also allows the social worker to think more openly and flexibly about the situation they are working with, to explore different ideas and perspectives and to seek help when needed.

  The whole team can also act as a secure base when team members are appropriately available to each other, either face to face or virtually. Colleagues who are approachable, open, consistent and honest in their communication help the social worker to feel that "people are there for me" in the team, particularly welcome and needed when dealing with a complex piece of work.

- **Sensitivity – helps to manage feelings**
  Moving a child to adoption can involve the full range of positive and difficult feelings for all involved in the process. The social worker will need to be sensitive to the emotions of the people they are working with and there may be times when these feelings are unexpectedly painful. The reflective space provided by a supervisor can be key in helping the social worker to think about what the child, the foster carers and the adopters might be thinking and feeling through the three stages of

the move, and whether the moving plan might need to be reviewed to accommodate this.

It is common for social workers to experience a range of feelings (perhaps excitement, apprehension, relief or frustration) during the moving period. The social worker's feelings might reflect those of the foster carers, adopters or child with whom they are working closely, or they might be wholly personal. In all cases, sensitive supervision can help the social worker to identify, understand and manage their feeling appropriately and to consider whether or not they are influencing the case planning.

In general terms, social workers feel supported by colleagues who demonstrate empathy, for example, by noticing and validating other people's feelings, offering advice or opportunities to talk, and by a team culture in which talking about feelings is viewed as necessary and helpful.

- **Acceptance – builds self-esteem**
Moving a child to adoption can involve a particularly intense period of work, requiring physical and emotional energy and a high level of skill. Social workers benefit from a supervisor who shows respect and appreciation of their work. This helps to build the social worker's professional confidence and also promotes resilience, which can help the worker to manage disappointments and setbacks.

The team culture can also contribute to the individual's positive self-esteem. For example, practice wisdom may be shared and achievements celebrated through team case discussions. At the same time, it may also be beneficial for the team to discuss difficult cases in an open and non-judgemental way, establishing an acceptance that setbacks are sometimes inevitable and that they can be worked through.

- **Co-operation – builds effectiveness**
A co-operative working relationship between the social worker and their supervisor is essential in navigating the difficult territory of supporting a child's move. Within this relationship, the social worker should feel that their observations, assessments and ideas are valued and respected, and that they can work together with their supervisor to achieve a shared goal. This helps to build competence and effectiveness.

The whole team can also contribute to a successful move through co-operative working relationships, with colleagues willing to cover tasks and stand in for each other when necessary. Team members who work together to provide direction and support each other feel confident that solutions to problems will be found. This helps alleviate feelings of isolation, which can be a source of stress.

- **Team membership – builds a sense of belonging**
  A sense of shared team identity and culture helps team members to feel a sense of belonging, mutual support, shared goals and values. This can help to create a positive and hopeful outlook around each child's move and be supportive and sustaining when there are difficulties.

This fifth and final dimension, team membership, emphasises the significance of the partnerships and collaboration that have informed the development of the UEA Moving to Adoption model. Open communication and a culture of mutually respectful and sensitive relationships can best support the child's pathway from their foster family into their new life in their adoptive family. The quality of the culture that supports these relationships should be a clear focus at all levels of the organisation.

References

Ainsworth MS, Bell S and Stayton D (1971) 'Individual differences in strange-situation behaviour of one year olds', in Schaffer H (ed) *The Origins of Human Social Relations*, New York: Academic Press

Ainsworth MS, Blehar M, Waters E and Wall S (1978) *Patterns of Attachment: A psychological study of the Strange Situation*, Hillsdale, NJ: Lawrence Erlbaum

Aldgate J and Simmonds J (eds) (1988) *Direct Work with Children*, London: BAAF

Argent H (2007) *Josh and Jaz have Three Mums*, London: BAAF

Argent H (2012) *Moving Pictures*, London: BAAF

Beckett S (2021) *Beyond Together or Apart: Planning for, assessing and placing sibling groups* (2nd edn), London: CoramBAAF

Biggart L, Ward E, Cook L and Schofield G (2017) 'The team as a secure base: promoting resilience and competence in child and family social work', *Children and Youth Services Review*, 83, pp. 119–130

Blackmore J, Burns G, Waters CS and Shelton KH (2020) '"The very first thing that connected us to him": adopters' experiences of sharing photographs, "talking" albums and other materials with their children prior to meeting', *Adoption & Fostering*, 44:3, pp. 225–241

Blythe S, Wilkes L and Halcomb E (2014) 'The foster carer's experience: an integrative review', *Collegian*, 21: 21032

Boswell S and Cudmore L (2014) '"The children were fine": acknowledging complex feelings in the move from foster care to adoption', *Adoption & Fostering*, 38:1, pp. 5–21

Bowlby J (1951) *Maternal Care and Mental Health*, Geneva: WHO

Bowlby J (1969) *Attachment and Loss: Volume I, Attachment*, London: Hogarth Press

Bowlby J (1980) *Attachment and Loss: Volume III, Loss, sadness and depression*, London: Hogarth Press

Breier A, Kelsoe JR, Kirwin PD, Beller SA, Wolkowitz OM and Pickar D (1988) 'Early parental loss and development of adult psychopathology', *Archives of General Psychiatry*, 45:11, pp. 987–93

Browning A (2015) 'Undertaking planned transitions for children in out-of-home care', *Adoption & Fostering*, 39:1, pp. 51–61

Burnell A, Castell K and Cousins G (2009) *Planning Transitions for Children Moving to Permanent Placement: What do you do after you say "hello"?*, London: Family Futures

Camis J (2001) *My Life and Me*, London: BAAF

Care Review Scotland (2020) *Independent Care Review: The promise*, available at: https://www.carereview.scot/wp-content/uploads/2020/02/The-Promise.pdf

CoramBAAF (2017) *Best Practice in Meetings between Prospective Adopters and Children prior to Matching*, Practice Note 64, London: CoramBAAF

Corrigan M and Moore J (2011) *Listening to Children's Wishes and Feelings: A training programme*, London: BAAF

Daniel D (2009) *Finding a Family for Tommy*, London: BAAF

Department for Education (2013) *Statutory Guidance on Adoption*, London: DfE

Dibben E with Butcher L and Upright H (2018) *Think Siblings Project: Messages for practice when assessing the needs of siblings for permanent placement and supporting siblings in adoptive families*, available at: www.coram.org.uk/thinksiblings

Dozier M, Grasso D, Lindhiem O and Lewis E (2011) 'The role of caregiver commitment in foster care: insights from the This Is my Baby Interview', in Oppenheim D and Goldsmith D (eds) *Attachment Theory in Clinical Work with Children: Bridging the gap between research and practice*, New York, NY: Guilford Press, pp. 90–109

Dozier M, Lindheim O and Akerman JP (2005) 'Attachment and bio-behavioural catch-up' in Berlin L, Ziv Y, Amaya-Jackson L and Greenberg MT (eds) *Enhancing Early Attachments*, New York, NY: Guilford Press

Edelstein S, Burge D and Waterman J (2001) 'Helping foster parents cope with separation, loss and grief', *Child Welfare*, LXXX: 1, pp. 5–25

Fahlberg V (1994) *A Child's Journey through Placement*, London: BAAF

Foli K (2009) 'Depression in adoptive parents: a model of understanding through Grounded Theory', *Western Journal of Nursing Research*, 32:3, pp. 379–400

Fursland E and Betts B (2015) *Organising an Adoption Activity Day*, London: BAAF

Gauthier Y, Fortin G and Jeʹliu G (2004) 'Clinical application of attachment theory in permanency planning for children in foster care: the importance of continuity of care', *Infant Mental Health Journal*, 25:4, pp. 379–396

Gilligan R (2009) *Promoting Resilience: Supporting children and young people who are in care, adopted or in need*, London: BAAF

Goffman E (1963) *Stigma: Notes on the management of spoiled identity*, London: Penguin

Griffiths J and Pilgrim T (2007) *Picnic in the Park*, London: BAAF

Hammond S and Cooper N (2013) *Digital Life Story Work: Using technology to help young people make sense of their experiences*, London: BAAF

Hindle D and Shulman G (eds) (2008) *The Emotional Experience of Adoption: A psychoanalytic perspective*, London: Routledge

Höjer I, Sebba J and Luke N (2013) *The Impact of Fostering on Foster Carers' Children: An international literature review*, Oxford: Rees Centre for Research in Fostering and Education, University of Oxford

Howe D (1998) *Patterns of Adoption: Nature, nurture and psychosocial development*, Oxford: Blackwell Science

Howe D (2011) *Attachment across the Lifecourse: A brief introduction*, London: Macmillan Education

Iyer P, Boddy J, Hammelsbeck R and Lynch-Huggins S (2020) *Contact following Placement in Care, Adoption, or Special Guardianship: Implications for children and young people's well-being. Evidence review*, London: Nuffield Family Justice Observatory

Jones C and Henderson G (2017) *Supporting Sibling Relationships of Children in Permanent Fostering and Adoptive Families*, Research Briefing 1, Strathclyde: University of Strathclyde

Kahn H (2003) *Tyler's Wishes*, London: BAAF

Kirton D (2001) 'Love, money and the fostering task', *Child & Family Social Work*, 6:3, pp. 119–208

Lanyado M (2003) The emotional tasks of moving from fostering to adoption: transitions, attachment, separation and loss, *Clinical Child Psychology and Psychiatry*, 8:3, pp. 337–349

Lewis L (2018) 'Meeting my child for the first time: adoptive parents' experiences of the period of adoption transition', *Adoption & Fostering*, 42:1, pp. 38–48

Logan J (1996) 'Birth mothers and their mental health: unchartered territory', *British Journal of Social Work*, 26, pp. 609–625

Lynes D and Sitoe A (2019) 'Disenfranchised grief: the emotional impact experienced by foster carers on the cessation of a placement', *Adoption & Fostering*, 43:1, pp. 22–34

Maye J (2011) *Me and my Family*, London: BAAF

Meakings S, Ottaway H, Coffey A, Palmer C, Doughty J and Shelton K (2018) 'The support needs and experiences of newly formed adoptive families: findings from the Wales Adoption Study', *Adoption & Fostering*, 42:1, pp. 58–75

Merchant E (2010) *Dad David, Baba Chris and Me*, London: BAAF

Mermarnia N, Nolte L, Norris C and Harborne A (2015) '"It felt like it was night all the time": listening to the experiences of birth mothers whose children have been taken into care or adopted', *Adoption & Fostering*, 39:4, pp. 303–317

Moffatt F (2020) *Writing a Later Life Letter* (2nd edn), London: CoramBAAF

Neil E (2010) 'The benefits and challenges of direct post-adoption contact: perspectives from adoptive parents and birth relatives', *Aloma: Revista de Psicologia, Ciències de l'Educacio i de l'Esport*, 27: pp. 89–115

Neil E and Beek M (2020) 'Respecting children's relationships and identities in adoption', in Wrobel G, Helder E and Marr E (eds), *The Routledge Handbook of Adoption*, London: Routledge, Taylor & Francis Group, pp. 76–89

Neil E, Beek M and Schofield G (2018) *Moving to Adoption: A practice development project*, *Research Briefings*, Norwich: Centre for Research on Children and Families, University of East Anglia

Neil E, Cossar J, Lorgelly P and Young J (2010) *Helping Birth Families: Services, costs and outcomes*, London: BAAF

Neil E, Morciano M, Young J and Hartley L (2020) 'Exploring links between early adversities and later outcomes for children adopted from care: implications for planning post adoption support', *Developmental Child Welfare*, 2:1, pp. 52–71

Neil E, Young J and Hartley L (2018) *The Joys and Challenges of Adoptive Family Life: A survey of adoptive parents in the Yorkshire and Humberside region*, Norwich: Centre for Research on Children and Families, UEA

Palacios J, Adroher S, Brodzinsky DM, Grotevant HD, Johnson DE, Juffer F, Martínez-Mora L, Muhamedrahimov RJ, Selwyn J, Simmonds J and Tarren-Sweeney M (2019) 'Adoption in the service of child protection: an international interdisciplinary perspective', *Psychology, Public Policy, and Law*, 25:2, pp. 57–72

Pyman M (2007) *Short-Term Fostering of Infants: Foster carers' experiences*, unpublished PhD thesis: University of East Anglia

Rees J (2017) *Life Story Books for Adopted and Fostered Children*, London: Jessica Kingsley Publications

Riggs DW and Willsmore S (2012) 'Experiences of disenfranchised grief arising from the unplanned termination of a foster placement: an exploratory South Australian study', *Adoption & Fostering*, 36:2, pp. 57–66

Robertson C (2018a) *Two Mums*, London: Sparklypoo Publications

Robertson C (2018b) *Two Dads*, London: Sparklypoo Publications

Robertson C (2018c) *Two Mums and a Menagerie*, London: Sparklypoo Publications

Robertson J and Robertson J (1989) *Separation and the Very Young*, London: Free Association Books

Rutter M (1971) 'Parent-child separation: psychological effects on the children', *Journal of Child Psychology and Psychiatry*, 12, pp. 233–260

Rutter M (1979) 'Maternal deprivation, 1972–1978: new findings, new concepts, new approaches', *Child Development*, 50:2, pp. 283–305

Ryan M (2020) *Contact between Children in Care or Adopted and their Families: Six key messages from research*, London: Nuffield Family Justice Observatory

Ryan T and Walker R (2016) *Life Story Work*, London: CoramBAAF

Schofield G (2005) 'The voice of the child in family placement decision making', *Adoption & Fostering*, 29:1, pp. 29–44

Schofield G and Beek M (2005) 'Providing a secure base: parenting children in long-term foster family care', *Attachment & Human Development*, 7:1, pp. 3–25

Schofield G and Beek M (2009) 'Growing up in foster care: providing a secure base in adolescence', *Child & Family Social Work*, 14, pp. 255–266

Schofield G and Beek M (2014a) *The Secure Base Model: Promoting attachment and resilience in foster care and adoption*, London: BAAF

Schofield G and Beek M (2014b) *Promoting Attachment and Resilience: a guide for foster carers and adopters on using the Secure Base model*, London: BAAF

Schofield G and Beek M (2018) *Attachment Handbook for Foster Care and Adoption* (2nd edn), London: CoramBAAF

Schofield G, Beek M, Biggart L and Ward E (2013) 'Professional foster carer and committed parent: role conflict and role enrichment at the interface between work and family in long-term foster care', *Child and Family Social Work*, 18:1, pp. 46–56

Schofield G, Moldesta B, Hojer I, Ward E, Skilbred D, Young J and Havik T (2011) 'Managing loss and a threatened identity: experiences of the parents of children growing up in foster care and implications for social work practice', *British Journal of Social Work*, 41:1, pp. 74–92

Selwyn J, Meakings S and Wijedasa D (2015) *Beyond the Adoption Order: Challenges, interventions and adoption disruption*, London: BAAF

Senecky Y, Hanoch A, Inbar D, Horesh N, Diamond G and Bergman YS (2009) 'Post-adoption depression among adoptive mothers', *Journal of Affective Disorders*, 115, pp. 62–68

Shah S and Argent H (2006) *Life Story Work: Why, what, how and when*, London: BAAF

Sims DL (2020) 'Encounters with liminality: transformative practices in the building of an adoptive family', *Journal of Social Work Practice*, pp. 1–14

Stovall C and Dozier M (2004) 'Forming attachments in foster care: infant attachment behaviours during the first two months of placement', *Development and Psychopathology*, 02, pp. 253–271

Sunderland M (2003) *Helping Children with Feelings* (resource pack), Bicester: Speechmark Publishing

Sydney L and Price E (2014) *Meaningful Contact in Adoption and Fostering*, London: Jessica Kingsley Publications

Thomas C (2013) *Adoption for Looked After Children: Messages from research, an overview of the Adoption Research Initiative*, London: BAAF

Thomas C, Beckford V, Lowe NV and Murch M (1999) *Adopted Children Speaking*, London: BAAF

Winkler R and van Keppel M (1984) *Relinquishing Mothers in Adoption: Their long term adjustment*, Melbourne: Institute of Family Studies

Appendix 1: Secure Base developmental checklist

Many children in foster care will have built trust in their foster carers as a secure base from which they can explore, learn and enjoy their world. For some infants, placed from birth, this will have been their only experience of caregiving and their trust will be deeply rooted. For other children, earlier experiences of separation or neglectful or abusive caregiving may cause them to remain anxious and to distrust close relationships or to be vulnerable to further separation.

When children move from foster care to adoption, it is important to note and understand the extent to which they have developed secure base relationships with their foster carers. Information about these relationships and the child's emotional development can feed in to the moving process and support the development of secure base relationships in the adoptive family.

These checklists are age-related, and correspond with the child's behaviours under five headings that are important elements of children's secure base relationships and emotional development:

- Trust
- Managing feelings
- Self-esteem
- Feeing effective
- Sense of belonging

NB. There are major changes to children's behaviours within each age range, and answers to some questions will depend on the specific age of the child. There are also differences (observable from birth) in levels of sociability and activity due to differences in temperament. The full range of normal development should, therefore, be taken into account.

These checklists should be used as a helpful source of information, not as an assessment tool.

Infants aged 0–18 months

Availability – helping the child to trust

Does the child:

- seek comfort when distressed (e.g. crying, gazing towards or (if mobile) approaching the caregiver)?

  ☐ Yes ☐ Sometimes ☐ No

- accept comfort when distressed (e.g. settling when picked up and cuddled)?

  ☐ Yes ☐ Sometimes ☐ No

- use a caregiver as a secure base for exploration (i.e. after accepting reassurance or comfort, become able to explore and play)?

  ☐ Yes ☐ Sometimes ☐ No

- show some degree of preference for one or more caregiver (e.g. gaze/ preferred for cuddles – develops during the first eight months)?

  ☐ Yes ☐ Sometimes ☐ No

- target attachment behaviours at this caregiver/these caregivers (e.g. gaze, verbalisation when upset/happy – approach once mobile)?

  ☐ Yes ☐ Sometimes ☐ No

- protest at separation from specific caregivers (range of protest – depending on temperament/attachment pattern)?

  ☐ Yes ☐ Sometimes ☐ No

- settle/settle to play at reunion?

  ☐ Yes ☐ Sometimes ☐ No

- show interest and pleasure in objects and things around them?

  ☐ Yes ☐ Sometimes ☐ No

- enjoy playing independently with objects/toys?

  ☐ Yes ☐ Sometimes ☐ No

- enjoy playing jointly with objects/toys?

  ☐ Yes ☐ Sometimes ☐ No

- "take turns" with/"converse" with adults – initiating and responding to vocalising, facial movements (can start from soon after birth)?

  ☐ Yes ☐ Sometimes ☐ No

> **Recent examples of these behaviours (to illustrate strengths *and* difficulties)**

> **Any additional comments**

Sensitivity – helping the child to manage feelings

Does the child:

- show a full range of positive emotions (e.g. smile, laugh, show pleasure)?

  ☐ Yes ☐ Sometimes ☐ No

- communicate their needs (e.g. for proximity, food, play)?

  ☐ Yes ☐ Sometimes ☐ No

- react appropriately to sensory stimuli (e.g. show interest/react positively or negatively, as appropriate, to light, sound, smell, touch, taste – but not overreact/panic or freeze)?

  ☐ Yes ☐ Sometimes ☐ No

- wait for attention/manage emotions – with help (e.g. voice of caregiver indicating food is on the way)?

  ☐ Yes ☐ Sometimes ☐ No

- sleep regularly and in a relaxed way/accept reassurance if wakes (NB sleep patterns will vary)?

  ☐ Yes ☐ Sometimes ☐ No

- seem comfortable in their body (e.g. able to relax and also enjoy being active)?

  ☐ Yes ☐ Sometimes ☐ No

- cope with being told 'no' (e.g. protest but then settle fairly quickly)?

  ☐ Yes ☐ Sometimes ☐ No

> **Recent examples of these behaviours (to illustrate strengths *and* difficulties)**

Any additional comments

Acceptance – building the child's self-esteem

Does the child:

- express pleasure at their achievements (e.g. shaking a rattle to make a noise, standing up on their own, building a tower)?

  ☐ Yes ☐ Sometimes ☐ No

- show interest and enthusiasm for interactive games like peek-a-boo (e.g. showing pleasure at success)?

  ☐ Yes ☐ Sometimes ☐ No

- approach new people/situations positively (balancing curiosity, caution and pleasurable anticipation)?

  ☐ Yes ☐ Sometimes ☐ No

- cope with setbacks (e.g. when the rattle doesn't work, the brick tower falls over)?

  ☐ Yes ☐ Sometimes ☐ No

Recent examples of these behaviours (to illustrate strengths *and* difficulties)

Any additional comments

Co-operation – helping the child to feel effective

Does the child:

- make choices (e.g. between foods, toys)?

  ☐ Yes ☐ Sometimes ☐ No

- assert themself (e.g. getting attention, feeding at their own pace)?

  ☐ Yes ☐ Sometimes ☐ No

- seem keen to try new things (NB some variation in enjoying novelty due to differences in temperament)?

☐ Yes   ☐ Sometimes   ☐ No

- show focus and persistence in their activities or play (e.g. sustained activity to complete task)?

☐ Yes   ☐ Sometimes   ☐ No

- co-operate with nappy changes, feeding, going to sleep (i.e. relaxing and accepting events with the reassurance of caregivers)?

☐ Yes   ☐ Sometimes   ☐ No

- play co-operatively (e.g. turn-taking/accepting support to hold the rattle, press the button to make a sound, can lead to co-operative play even in infancy)?

☐ Yes   ☐ Sometimes   ☐ No

Recent examples of these behaviours (to illustrate strengths *and* difficulties)

Any additional comments

Family membership – helping the child to belong to the current caregiving family

Does the child:

- recognise family members and extended family members?

☐ Yes   ☐ Sometimes   ☐ No

- prefer family members and family friends (e.g. more likely to communicate with/accept cuddles from)?

☐ Yes   ☐ Sometimes   ☐ No

- enjoy family occasions (e.g. seem to fit in as part of the family – if supported/not overwhelmed)?

☐ Yes   ☐ Sometimes   ☐ No

Recent examples of these behaviours (to illustrate strengths *and* difficulties)

> **Any additional comments**

Family membership – helping the child to belong to the birth family

Does the child:

- recognise birth family members and extended birth family members?

  ☐ Yes ☐ Sometimes ☐ No

- interact positively with birth family members (e.g. communicates with/ accepts cuddles from)?

  ☐ Yes ☐ Sometimes ☐ No

- enjoy birth family contact time (if supported/not overwhelmed)?

  ☐ Yes ☐ Sometimes ☐ No

> **Recent examples of these behaviours (to illustrate strengths *and* difficulties)**

> **Any additional comments**

Child aged 19 months–4 years

Availability – helping the child to trust

Does the child:

- seek comfort when distressed (e.g. signal their needs verbally or physically, rather than shut down on feelings; demand then resist comfort; appear helpless; try to control others)?

  ☐ Yes ☐ Sometimes ☐ No

- accept comfort when stressed, then relax and settle?

  ☐ Yes ☐ Sometimes ☐ No

- use a caregiver as a secure base for exploration (i.e. after accepting reassurance or comfort, become able to explore and play)?

☐ Yes ☐ Sometimes ☐ No

- have a selective attachment to one or more caregivers?

  ☐ Yes ☐ Sometimes ☐ No

- protest at separation from primary caregiver/s (there will be a range of protest behaviours depending on temperament/attachment pattern)?

  ☐ Yes ☐ Sometimes ☐ No

- settle to play at reunion with caregiver?

  ☐ Yes ☐ Sometimes ☐ No

- show interest and pleasure in objects and things around them?

  ☐ Yes ☐ Sometimes ☐ No

- enjoy playing independently with toys?

  ☐ Yes ☐ Sometimes ☐ No

- enjoy playing jointly with toys?

  ☐ Yes ☐ Sometimes ☐ No

- use their mobility and language to explore, have fun, approach others, to learn?

  ☐ Yes ☐ Sometimes ☐ No

Recent examples of these behaviours (to illustrate strengths *and* difficulties)

Any additional comments

Sensitivity – helping the child to manage feelings

Does the child:

- express a range of positive feelings (excitement, pleasure, delight) but not be overwhelmed by them?

  ☐ Yes ☐ Sometimes ☐ No

- express a range of negative feelings (anger, disappointment, sadness) but not be overwhelmed by them?

  ☐ Yes ☐ Sometimes ☐ No

- name simple feelings?

  ☐ Yes   ☐ Sometimes   ☐ No

- use language to communicate needs, feelings, ideas and goals openly and accurately (appropriate to their age)?

  ☐ Yes   ☐ Sometimes   ☐ No

- ever pretend to feel what they are not feeling, e.g. smile when anxious (this can start as young as 18 months)?

  ☐ Yes   ☐ Sometimes   ☐ No

- understand that others have thoughts, feelings and goals that differ from their own?

  ☐ Yes   ☐ Sometimes   ☐ No

- show empathy for others?

  ☐ Yes   ☐ Sometimes   ☐ No

- show some understanding of acceptable and unacceptable behaviour (moral development)?

  ☐ Yes   ☐ Sometimes   ☐ No

Recent examples of these behaviours (to illustrate strengths *and* difficulties)

Any additional comments

Acceptance – building the child's self-esteem

Does the child:

- enjoy play and activities?

  ☐ Yes   ☐ Sometimes   ☐ No

- take pleasure in doing something well?

  ☐ Yes   ☐ Sometimes   ☐ No

- enjoy praise?

  ☐ Yes   ☐ Sometimes   ☐ No

- cope with setbacks (e.g. not managing a task, not winning a game sometimes)?

  ☐ Yes ☐ Sometimes ☐ No

  Recent examples of these behaviours (to illustrate strengths *and* difficulties)

  Any additional comments

Co-operation – helping the child to feel effective

Does the child:

- make simple choices?

  ☐ Yes ☐ Sometimes ☐ No

- show persistence in completing tasks?

  ☐ Yes ☐ Sometimes ☐ No

- co-operate and negotiate?

  ☐ Yes ☐ Sometimes ☐ No

- show focus and persistence in setbacks (e.g. not managing a task, not winning a game sometimes)?

  ☐ Yes ☐ Sometimes ☐ No

- manage increased independence without excessive assertiveness/ oppositional behaviour?

  ☐ Yes ☐ Sometimes ☐ No

- enjoy/manage sleeping, eating, toileting, appropriate for age?

  ☐ Yes ☐ Sometimes ☐ No

- manage peer relationships (e.g. prosocial, increasingly co-operative, making and keeping friends)?

  ☐ Yes ☐ Sometimes ☐ No

> **Recent examples of these behaviours (to illustrate strengths *and* difficulties)**

> **Any additional comments**

Family membership – helping the child to belong to the current caregiving family

Does the child:

- recognise current caregiving family members and extended family members?

  ☐ Yes ☐ Sometimes ☐ No

- show some preference for familiar family members and family friends (e.g. more likely to communicate with/accept cuddles from)?

  ☐ Yes ☐ Sometimes ☐ No

- enjoy family occasions (e.g. seem to fit in as part of the family – if supported/not overwhelmed)?

  ☐ Yes ☐ Sometimes ☐ No

> **Recent examples of these behaviours (to illustrate strengths *and* difficulties)**

> **Any additional comments**

Child aged 5–10 years

Availability – helping the child to trust

Does the child:

- seek comfort/help from others appropriately (when needed but not excessively – balancing dependency and autonomy)?

137

☐ Yes   ☐ Sometimes   ☐ No

- have selective attachment to specific caregiver/s?

☐ Yes   ☐ Sometimes   ☐ No

- use a caregiver as a secure base for exploration (i.e. seek comfort, have anxiety reduced, then explore/learn/play)?

☐ Yes   ☐ Sometimes   ☐ No

- trust people outside the family appropriately, e.g. teachers, activity leaders, peer group?

☐ Yes   ☐ Sometimes   ☐ No

- indiscriminately seek out/show affection to others?

☐ Yes   ☐ Sometimes   ☐ No

- manage friendships with peers successfully?

☐ Yes   ☐ Sometimes   ☐ No

Recent examples of these behaviours (to illustrate strengths *and* difficulties)

Any additional comments

Sensitivity – helping the child to manage feelings

Does the child:

- express a range of positive feelings (excitement, pleasure, delight) but not be overwhelmed by them?

☐ Yes   ☐ Sometimes   ☐ No

- express a range of negative feelings (anger, disappointment, sadness) but not be overwhelmed by them?

☐ Yes   ☐ Sometimes   ☐ No

- communicate their feelings accurately in ways that can get their needs met?

☐ Yes   ☐ Sometimes   ☐ No

- talk about/reflect on their feelings?

☐ Yes ☐ Sometimes ☐ No

- talk about/reflect on the feelings of other people?

  ☐ Yes ☐ Sometimes ☐ No

- show empathy for other children?

  ☐ Yes ☐ Sometimes ☐ No

- show more complex emotions of guilt, shame or remorse?

  ☐ Yes ☐ Sometimes ☐ No

- understand and accept the rules at home?

  ☐ Yes ☐ Sometimes ☐ No

- understand and accept the rules at school?

  ☐ Yes ☐ Sometimes ☐ No

- have effective strategies for managing their feelings and behaviour?

  ☐ Yes ☐ Sometimes ☐ No

Recent examples of these behaviours (to illustrate strengths *and* difficulties)

Any additional comments

Acceptance – building the child's self-esteem

Does the child:

- have positive self-esteem – think they are good at things and able to accept not being good at others?

  ☐ Yes ☐ Sometimes ☐ No

- respond positively to praise at home or at school?

  ☐ Yes ☐ Sometimes ☐ No

- take pride in their appearance?

  ☐ Yes ☐ Sometimes ☐ No

- feel positive about their school performance?

  ☐ Yes ☐ Sometimes ☐ No

- get involved in and enjoy activities or hobbies?

  ☐ Yes ☐ Sometimes ☐ No

- enjoy peer group relationships/cope with the stresses?

  ☐ Yes ☐ Sometimes ☐ No

- cope with setbacks and disappointment?

  ☐ Yes ☐ Sometimes ☐ No

- cope with being told off, i.e. not despairing, shutting down or becoming aggressive?

  ☐ Yes ☐ Sometimes ☐ No

Recent examples of these behaviours (to illustrate strengths *and* difficulties)

Any additional comments

Co-operation – helping the child to feel effective

Does the child:

- make choices?

  ☐ Yes ☐ Sometimes ☐ No

- assert themselves appropriately?

  ☐ Yes ☐ Sometimes ☐ No

- feel effective and competent?

  ☐ Yes ☐ Sometimes ☐ No

- follow through and complete tasks?

  ☐ Yes ☐ Sometimes ☐ No

- look after their things appropriately?

  ☐ Yes ☐ Sometimes ☐ No

- enjoy co-operation with others/can negotiate?

  ☐ Yes ☐ Sometimes ☐ No

> **Recent examples of these behaviours (to illustrate strengths *and* difficulties)**

> **Any additional comments**

Family membership – helping the child to belong to the current caregiving family

Does the child:

- seem comfortable spending time with the current caregiving family?
  ☐ Yes   ☐ Sometimes   ☐ No

- seem willing/happy to be involved in family events?
  ☐ Yes   ☐ Sometimes   ☐ No

- enjoy family occasions (e.g. seem to fit in as part of the family – if supported/not overwhelmed)?
  ☐ Yes   ☐ Sometimes   ☐ No

> **Recent examples of these behaviours (to illustrate strengths *and* difficulties)**

> **Any additional comments**

Family membership – helping the child to belong to the birth family

Does the child:

- see themselves as part of/connected to their birth family (appropriate to placement type)?
  ☐ Yes   ☐ Sometimes   ☐ No

- talk about the birth family in a balanced way?

☐ Yes ☐ Sometimes ☐ No

- tell a coherent story of their childhood and birth family life that makes sense to them and is realistic?

☐ Yes ☐ Sometimes ☐ No

- enjoy birth family contact (if supported)?

☐ Yes ☐ Sometimes ☐ No

Recent examples of these behaviours (to illustrate strengths *and* difficulties)

Any additional comments

Appendix 2: Caregiving approaches with the child

CAREGIVING APPROACHES FOR HELPING THE CHILD TO BUILD TRUST

Day-to-day caregiving

- Establish predictable routines around mealtimes, getting up and going to bed. Make these explicit to the child and talk them through in advance.

- Use a calendar or picture chart to help the child predict and anticipate events.

- Ensure that the child feels specially cared for and nurtured when ill, hurt or sad.

- Be unobtrusively available if the child is anxious but finds it hard to talk or accept comfort (for example, sit nearby, suggest a ride in the car).

- Offer verbal and non-verbal support for safe exploration.

- Respond promptly to the child's signals for support or comfort or reassure an older child that you will respond as promised as soon as possible. For example: 'I must quickly finish what I am doing and then I will come and help you straight away'.

Building trust when caregiver and child are apart

- Manage separations carefully, with open communication about why it is happening, how long it will be, and clear "goodbyes" and "hellos".

- Ensure that the child always knows how to contact you when you are apart.

- Allow the child to take a small item or photo from home to school.

- Use your mobile phone to ring or text to help the child know that you are thinking of them.

- Place a small surprise on the child's bed when they are at school. Tell them that you have done this because you have thought about them during the day.

- Keep a "goodies tub" in the kitchen and put small treats in it for the child to have in the evening. Tell them that you have done this because you have thought about them during the day.

Games and activities

- Ask the child to draw a fortress or make one in clay or sand. The child may choose miniature toys or animals to stand for the main people in their life. Ask the child to show and talk about which ones they would let into their fort and which ones they would keep out and why (from Sunderland, 2003).

- Ask the child to draw a bridge with themselves on one side and someone they trust on the other. Ask them to draw a speech bubble coming out of their mouth and write in it what they are thinking or saying. Do the same with the other person (from Sunderland, 2003).

CAREGIVING APPROACHES FOR HELPING THE CHILD TO MANAGE FEELINGS

Day-to-day caregiving

- Observe the child carefully – keep a diary, note patterns, the unexpected, try to stand in the child's shoes. Gently feed back observations to the child, as appropriate.

- Anticipate what will cause confusion and distress for the child and avoid if possible.

- Express interest, at a level that is comfortable for the child, in their thoughts and feelings.

- Provide shared, pleasurable activity and a "commentary" on the feelings experienced by yourself and the child.

- Encourage the child to *stop* and *think* before reacting.

- Help the child recover/repair the situation/make things better after losing control of their feelings – praise them for doing this.

- Name and talk about feelings in everyday situations, e.g. 'Your friend is going on holiday tomorrow. I wonder how they are feeling?'.

- Reflect on events and relationships – discuss mixed feelings and feelings that change over time.

Games and activities

- Make a "My calendar" to help the child to see and remember/anticipate what will happen each day.

- Play "sensory" games (involving touch, sound, smell, taste, observation).

- Use clay, paint or crayons to help the child to express feelings.

- Use play to help the child to make sense of the world, how things work, cause and effect.

- Use stories or puppets to develop empathy in the child – 'Poor owl, how does he feel now his tree has been cut down?', etc.

- Use television programmes/films to help the child to focus on why people feel different things and how they can feel different things at the same time.

- Collect tickets, pictures, leaflets, stickers, etc, and discuss with the child their feelings about each event.

- Make an "experiences book" to help the child remember and reflect on positive events, and to understand the passage of time – past, present and anticipated future.

CAREGIVING APPROACHES FOR BUILDING THE CHILD'S SELF-ESTEEM

Day-to-day caregiving

- Praise the child for achieving small tasks and responsibilities.

- Provide toys and games that create a sense of achievement.

- Liaise closely with the child's nursery or school to ensure a sense of achievement.

- Use positive language. For example, 'Hold the cup tight – good, well done', rather than 'Don't drop the cup'.

- Offer the child a brief explanation of why behaviour is not acceptable and a clear indication of what is preferred. For example: 'If you shout, it's really hard for me to hear what you want to say. I want to be able to hear you, so please talk in an ordinary voice.'

- Use dolls, toys, games and books that promote a positive sense of the child's ethnic, religious and cultural background.

- Ensure that the child's ethnic, religious and cultural background is valued and celebrated within the household.

- Model the acceptance of difference in words and behaviour.

- Model a sense of pride in self and surroundings.

- Model within the family that it is OK not to be perfect, that 'no one is good at everything but everyone is good at something'.

Games and activities

- Help the child to list and think about all the things they have done that they feel proud of. Use photos and other mementos to record these events.

- List, alongside the child, all the things that make you feel proud of them. This can include acceptance of their limitations (e.g. a time when the child tried but did not succeed at something, was able to accept losing, etc).

- Encourage the child to draw, paint, make a clay model or play music to express how it feels when they feel good about themself. Do the same for yourself.

- As a family group, suggest that each person in the family writes down one good thing about all other family members, so that each child gets given a set of positive things about themselves.

- Make a poster with the child of "best achievements".

- Ask the child to teach you something that they are good at – such as a computer game or a joke.

- Discover and support activities and interests that the child enjoys and can be successful in. This may need active support (liaison with club leader, becoming a helper at the club, etc).

- Play rules-based games with the child, such as board games – help the child to manage feelings/enjoy the competition, whether winning or losing.

- With the child, draw a picture of the child – encourage the child to make positive statements about different parts of themself – shiny hair, pretty T-shirt, friendly smiles, feet good at kicking a ball – help the child to write them on the drawing and talk about them.

CAREGIVING APPROACHES FOR HELPING THE CHILD TO FEEL EFFECTIVE

Day-to-day caregiving

- Within the house and garden, minimise hazards and things that the child cannot touch, and keep "out of bounds" areas secure so that they can explore without adult "interference" when they are ready to do so.

- Make opportunities for choices. For example, allow the child to choose the cereal at the supermarket, a pudding for a family meal, or what to wear for a certain activity.

- Ensure that daily routines include time to relax together and share a pleasurable activity.

- Do not try to tackle several problem areas at any one time. Set one or two priorities and work on them gradually until there are sustained signs of progress. Ensure that these are acknowledged.

- Use co-operative language wherever possible. For example: 'Would you like to come and have a sandwich after you've washed your hands?', rather than 'Wash your hands before you eat your sandwich'.

Games and activities

- Suggest small tasks and responsibilities within the child's capabilities. Ensure recognition and praise when achieved. If tasks become an issue, do them alongside the child – this is a chance to show availability.

- Introduce toys where the action of the child achieves a rewarding result, for example, pushing a button, touching or shaking something.

- Find shared activities that the child enjoys and that produce a clear result, for example, baking cakes.

- Introduce games that promote co-operation, turn-taking and teamwork.

- Seek opportunities for the child to co-operate with other children – you may need to be present so that this is managed successfully.

- Find time for interactions that promote working together, for example, simple action rhymes and songs, clapping games, ball and beanbag games, learning a dance together, building or making something together, a shared "adventure" or new experience.

- Help the child/young person to identify a target that they would like to achieve, do, change, etc. Settle on one where something done now will make a difference. Discuss what they can do and negotiate simple, relevant and achievable steps that they can take. When agreed, draw a simple staircase and write one task on each of the steps of the staircase.

For example, if the target is 'Go to see the child's favourite football team play at home', steps might be: use the internet to find out dates of home games this season, settle on a suitable date and put on the calendar, find out train times, etc. Set a time to review progress and think about further steps needed.

CAREGIVING APPROACHES FOR HELPING THE CHILD TO BELONG

Belonging to the adoptive or foster family

- Explain to the child from the beginning how the family works – its routines and expectations, its choice of food and favourite television programmes – so that the child can see how to fit in.

- Adapt those routines where possible and reasonable to accommodate the child's norms and help them feel at home, e.g. mealtimes or bedtime.

- Have special places for the child in the home, e.g. a hook for the child's coat, a place at the table, bedding and bedroom decoration (posters, etc) that reflect the child's age and interests.

- Promote family mealtimes and activities (e.g. going bowling) where the child can feel fully accepted as part of the family.

- Ensure that extended family members and friends welcome the child and treat them as one of the family.

- Have photos of the child on display – alongside photos of other children in the family or who have lived in the family and moved on/grown up.

- Make an album of family experiences that have included the child. This can help the child to reflect on family life and, in a short-term placement, can be taken home to the birth family or to a new placement.

- Make sure the school knows (and the child knows that the school knows) that you are the family caring for the child and need to be kept informed of any concerns but also of achievements and events to celebrate.

- Talk about regular family activities that will include the child.

Being connected to the birth family

- Have photos of the child's birth family where they would most like to put them, e.g. in their bedroom, in a book, in the living room.

- Ensure that conversations about the birth family are carefully managed, so that the child does not have to make sense of negative, contradictory or idealised ideas about birth family members.

- Where direct or indirect contact is occurring, be actively involved in planning and facilitating contact so that the child's welfare is paramount and contact promotes security as well as roots and identity.

- Talk to the child's teacher about family issues that may unsettle the child, if raised in class.

Managing membership of more than one family

- Adults need to demonstrate their own flexibility about children's family memberships and what they might mean to the child.

- Both informally and in a planned way, talk with the child about the benefits and challenges of having more than one family and help them to understand and manage these relationships.

- Find models around the child of children who manage multiple families, e.g. in friends' families, on television, in books.

- Help the child to think about/talk about the inevitability of mixed feelings.

- Watch for possible pressure points, e.g. Mother's Day, Father's Day, or important festivals like Christmas or Eid, and find ways of indicating (where appropriate) that it is OK to give cards to more than one parent or to choose one rather than the other at different times.

- If necessary, talk to the child's teacher about family issues that may disturb the child if raised in class, i.e. help others outside the immediate family circle to be aware of the child's task in managing their multiple loyalties/families.

Appendix 3: Applying the UEA Moving to Adoption model – additional considerations in Scotland[7]

LEGAL AND POLICY FRAMEWORK

The care system in Scotland underwent a root-and-branch review in recent years, which resulted in the making of *The Promise* (Care Review, 2020).

Practice and policy in Scotland support the principles of the Moving to Adoption model. This is exemplified in the body of *The Promise* (p. 67):

> *If required, a stable, loving home must be found as quickly as possible. It is unacceptable to make children experience the number of moves many are required to make...Scotland must limit the number of moves that children experience and support carers to contribute to care...Any transition in a care experienced child's life must be limited, relational, planned and informed...Many care experienced children have told the Care Review how scary and upsetting transitions are and specifically that the transition away from their families was often badly managed.*

The focus of the guidance of the Looked After Children (Scotland) Regulations 2009 and the Adoption and Children (Scotland) Act 2007 is on the obligations and best practice of the local authority. There are a number of points in this guidance that align with the UEA Moving to Adoption model and key principles, in particular the focus in the Scottish guidance on (a) preparing and supporting children for the move and recognising and responding to their feelings; and (b) building in

---

7 These guidelines have been drafted in collaboration with Rhona Pollock, Legal Consultant, AFA Scotland.

continuity for the child, including continuity of relationships with the foster family:

It is important for good timing of the linking process to ensure that there is ongoing work with the child that enables them to begin to understand the plans that are being made and explores their views, however they may be able to express them. Moving a child into an adoptive placement when they are confused or hostile to the plan increases the potential for the placement to disrupt, so consideration of matching should take into account the timing of any link...The waiting period between the making of the plan for adoption and arranging the placement is not neutral. Children need simple explanations of what is happening and whether or not it is intended that they will return home. If they have been told it is not planned for them to return home, it is important to explain the purpose of any ongoing contact with birth relatives. Temporary foster carers often play a key role in this and may need support in how to respond to a child's concerns and in handling both their own and the child's distress. (p. 192)

Times of transition are particularly stressful for children – especially as so many of them have experienced multiple moves. Links with familiar people who supported them in foster care will be reassuring. The move itself may stir up thoughts and memories about the past which their social worker may be best placed to handle. A move into an adoption placement is usually carefully planned and should feel very different from any earlier experiences of sudden or unplanned moves. It is important therefore that during this period there is continuity for the child. It would normally be expected that the child's worker continues with this role following the move to adopters. This may be more difficult where it has been necessary to look further afield for adopters for a child. Where distance is a factor this may also be an added stress for the child who could feel abandoned in a strange area. Other ways of maintaining contact with the child's home area may be needed during the period of transition. (p. 197)

CHILDREN'S HEARING SYSTEM

The vast majority of children in Scotland who are in foster care are involved in the Children's Hearing System. There are three principles in law relating to Children's Hearings, which underpin the system:

- the welfare of the child is paramount;
- the child's views must be taken into account;
- no order should be made in relation to a child unless it is better to make an order than not to.

Therefore, decisions made by Hearings will need to reflect these principles.

Legal orders made by the Children's Hearing can secure the child's placement away from their birth parents. Children will be subject to compulsory supervision orders (CSOs) with a measure that they reside with named foster carers. To facilitate the move from foster carer to prospective adopter, a Children's Hearing would need to vary the CSO to name the prospective adopters' address as the child's new place of residence. Children's Hearings will not move a child simply because the local authority plan is to pursue for the child permanence away from home. In adapting and applying the UEA model, there is no suggestion that a decision will be made that pre-empts the decision of the court in terms of deciding on the permanence plan for the child; rather, where Children's Hearing Panel members decide that the CSO should be varied in the best interests of the child, that decision can be implemented in an effective and child-centred way.

APPLYING THE UEA MOVING TO ADOPTION MODEL IN SCOTLAND

A key difference in the application of the UEA Moving to Adoption model in Scotland is that only some Stage 1 activities can be undertaken prior to the Children's Hearing agreeing to the child's change of residence. The agreement of the Children's Hearing will be needed in order to begin regular meetings between the child and prospective adopters. Figure A1 below summarises how the UEA model can be applied in relation to the Children's Hearing system in Scotland.

Figure A1: Applying the UEA Moving to Adoption model to adoption in Scotland

Preliminary stages	Agreeing match between child and adopters – may include some limited "chemistry" meetings.
Stage 1 – Getting to know each other *Prior to Children's Hearing*	Begin Stage 1 activities building relationships between foster carers and adopters. Prepare for Hearing.
Stage 1 – Getting to know each other *After Children's Hearing*	Proceed with Stage 1 activities, building familiarity and trust between child and adopters through observation and play meetings.

Stage 2 – Making the move	Start intensive activities and visits preparing for adopters to care for the child full time. This stage finishes when the child moves to the adopters' address.
Stage 3 – Supporting relationships after the move	Support continuity of experiences and relationships after the move.

Preliminary stages

The use of "chemistry" or "bump-into" meetings has been developing in Scotland with the purpose of informing the match with prospective adopters. These should be clearly distinguished from Stage 1 meetings, where the purpose is to allow a gradual introduction between the child and the adopters, and the adopters are clearly introduced as such when they meet the child.

Stage 1 – Getting to know each other (prior to the Children's Hearing)

Once the match between the child and adopters has been agreed, meetings between the foster carers and adopters aimed at building a relationship between the adults, and increasing the adopters' understanding of the child's needs and routines, should be facilitated prior to attending a Children's Hearing. Information about the progress of these meetings would be included in the report submitted by the social worker to help inform the Hearing about the plan, without pre-empting any decision it might make.

The local authority will need to prepare for the Children's Hearing to enable the authorisation of the move to the adopters. Where the local authority seeks to move the child, the child's social worker will write to the Children's Reporter requiring a Children's Hearing to review the CSO because it "ought to be varied". Depending on the Hearing's diary, this may not take place for several weeks. Great care needs to be taken at this stage not to presume the outcome of the upcoming Hearing. Those who know the child – the current carers and the social worker in particular – will be sensitive to the needs of the child and how best to support them and manage their expectations.

In some instances, where a previous Children's Hearing has decided that it is not in the child's best interests, the child's place of residence will not be disclosed to those who would otherwise be entitled to this information (e.g. the child's parents). It may be that no such non-disclosure measure is attached to the current CSO, but the local authority may consider it necessary on moving the child to prospective adopters. Particular care should be taken in these situations and specifically addressed when the local authority is seeking to have the CSO reviewed.

At this stage, any request for non-disclosure of the adopters' address should be notified to the Children's Reporter. This should be confirmed by telephone. It is essential that this is clear because the Children's Reporter will send out all panel papers to the Relevant Persons and these will contain identifying information about the adopters.

The child's social worker will need to submit a report that will provide the Hearing with comprehensive information about the child and parents' circumstances, including reasons as to why a CSO remains necessary. The report will further state why moving the child to live with the prospective adopters is required. For the child to move to the adopters, the adopters will need to be dual approved as foster carers under the Looked After Children (Scotland) Regulations 2009. This provides the local authority with the authority to place the child with the adopters – who will be referred to as "the foster carers" in the Children's Hearing.

A Children's Hearing will be arranged and the child, Relevant Persons, current foster carers and prospective adopters should be invited by the Children's Reporter, along with the social worker and any other relevant professionals involved in the case.

The Hearing will move a child where it is established that this is in the child's best interest. Therefore, a recommendation to move the child will be based on evidenced information that the prospective adopters' care represents what is in the best interests of the child. Often, this Hearing will also be asked to give advice to the Sheriff in relation to the local authority's plans for permanence. These are two separate parts of the Hearing:

- The advice to the Sheriff will look at the reasons why adoption is required, based on, for example, the needs of the child, the circumstances of the parents, their care of the child and the likelihood of their being in a position to resume appropriate care of the child. Any advice provided to the Sheriff cannot be the subject of an appeal.

- The second part of that Hearing, namely the variation of the CSO, is a substantive decision and can therefore be appealed by the child, Relevant Persons and any Safeguarder.

Stage 1 – Getting to know each other (after the Children's Hearing)

Where the Children's Hearing decides that the CSO should be varied to name the adopters' home as the place of residence, the measure of residence will reflect this. The local authority may then begin the process of moving the child to live with the adopters. Moving the child should be done gradually and in line with the recommendations of the UEA Moving to Adoption model. This process will be predicated on the unfolding needs and reactions of the child. Building on the earlier meetings between the foster carers and adopters, the process of introducing the child to their prospective adopters through observation and play meetings can take place. There is no legal imperative for the child's move to be rushed; the legislation can be interpreted to allow for this necessary flexibility. There is nothing in the legislation that stipulates how soon the move has to happen or for how long the transition period will last. There is no minimum number of nights during which the child must live at the named place. However, the local authority is charged with implementing the Hearing's decision and should not indefinitely accommodate a child elsewhere from the address named on the CSO. The concern would be that if something happens when the child is not living at the address on the CSO, the local authority could be held responsible as the question might arise as to why the child was not residing at the place on the legal order.

Where the Hearing is made aware of the plan of gradual introductions and this is stated in their Reasons for Decision, it shows that the Hearing, in making its decision, understood that the child would continue living with their current carers until the transition period is completed.

Stage 2 – Making the move

Stage 2 will reflect the principles of the UEA model. It will begin when there are clear indications that the child is feeling familiar and comfortable with the adopters and when the foster carers and the adopters feel confident to proceed. Stage 2 is explored in Chapter 5 of this guide.

Stage 3 – Supporting relationships after the move

Best practice in Stage 3 will again reflect the principles of the UEA model. The child will continue to be a looked after child, and the adopters, as the child's legal foster carers, will be subject to the terms of the Looked After Children (Scotland) Regulations 2009. Stage 3 is explored in Chapter 6 of this guide.

Bestselling practical guides to understanding and using the Secure Base model – for social workers, foster carers and adopters

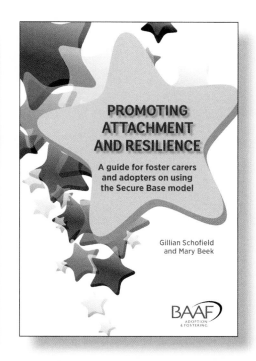

The Secure Base Model
£16.95

Promoting Attachment and Resilience using the Secure Base Model
£12.95

Bulk discounts available

Order from www.corambaaf.org.uk/books